Stepping Heavenward: A Bible Study Guide

Stepping Heavenward

A Bible Study Guide
Based on the Book
by
Elizabeth Prentiss

Compiled by

Carson Kistner

Solid Ground Christian Books
Birmingham, Alabama

Solid Ground Christian Books
PO Box 660132
Vestavia Hills AL 35266
205-443-0311
sgcb@charter.net
http://solid-ground-books.com

Stepping Heavenward: A Bible Study Guide

Compiled by Carson Kistner

Based on the book *Stepping Heavenward* by Elizabeth Prentiss published by Solid Ground Christian Books

Manufactured in the United States of America

Contents

Dear Friends,

Welcome to our Bible study based on Elizabeth Prentiss's classic, *Stepping Heavenward*. I believe that you are going to find our time together a life-changing journey as we glean precious treasures from God's Word and from the wisdom of this 19th century saint.

Although our heroine Katy Mortimer is a fictitious character, Mrs. Prentiss uses Katy's journal as a mouthpiece to convey profound truths that God has taught her as she has walked with Him. We will find ourselves reminiscing as Katy moves through her adolescent years. We will smile at her discovery the first month of marriage that "men are not like women." And we will empathize with her longings to be the perfect mother. We will rejoice with her in her victories and joys, and we will weep with her in her failures and sorrows. And along the way, as we seek God's face, He will enlighten the eyes of our hearts to the hope, the riches, and the power available for us as believers in the Lord Jesus Christ.

I have never met most of you in person, but I have prayed for you the prayer below that Paul prayed for the Ephesians. Come now as we travel together on an unforgettable journey.

Affectionately in Christ,

Carson Kistner

Carson Kistner
September 2003

(I) Cease not to give thanks for you, making mention of you in my prayers; That the God of our Lord Jesus Christ, the Father of glory, may give unto you the spirit of wisdom and revelation in the knowledge of him: The eyes of your understanding being enlightened; that ye may know what is the hope of his calling, and what the riches of the glory of his inheritance in the saints, And what is the exceeding greatness of his power to us-ward who believe, according to the working of his mighty power, . . . Ephesians 1:16-19a

A few instructions before you begin . . .

Materials you will need: Bible, Solid Ground Christian Books edition of *Stepping Heavenward*, this workbook, and a journal in which to record your memory verses and personal applications.

Each week you will begin by reading a portion of the story. The reading assignment is clearly designated on the title page of the lesson in this workbook and in the top right corner of each page of the lesson. After you read the assigned portion of the story, you will then work through the lesson in this workbook. Each lesson consists of four sections:

Memory Verse:

Beneath the lesson's title is a *suggested* Scripture memory verse. You may memorize the suggested verse, or you may select another verse to memorize that has been meaningful in your study. Whatever verse you choose, copy it into your journal, and begin working on it early in the week. Let's encourage each other to be diligent in our memorizing of Scripture.

Treasures from the Story:

This section highlights miscellaneous tidbits of God's truth that abound throughout the book. You are asked to look up a variety of Scripture verses and apply them specifically to the story.

The Bible Emphasis:

This section leads you into a more in-depth look at a particular theme that is illuminated in the story. We search God's Word together for a clear understanding of one subject. The lesson title gives you a hint as to what "The Bible Emphasis" is.

Personal Applications:

Each lesson concludes with two questions that clearly call you to action. You are to respond to the Holy Spirit's specific word to you by writing in your journal. By recording personal applications each week, you will have a complete record of what God is doing in your life and how you need to respond.

Note: All quotations from *Stepping Heavenward* found in this Bible study follow the pagination of the Solid Ground Christian Books edition.

Katy's Dilemma
(and Ours, Too!)

"Sin is the root of our misery; and therefore it is the proper work of (God's) mercy, to rescue the soul from it, both from the guilt and the power of it at once."
(Leighton 173)

Katy's Dilemma (and Ours, Too!)

For that which I do I allow not: for what I would, that do I not; but what I hate, that do I.
Romans 7:15

(This is your memory verse. Don't forget to copy it into your journal.)

Treasures from the Story

1. Handling the Praise of Men

Katy continually fails in following through with her resolutions made under her bed covers? (pp. 1, 6) What is her admitted motive for these resolutions? (p. 1) What is her definition of "a pretty good time at school"? (p. 2)

What do the following Scriptures tell us about the praise of men?

Proverbs 27:2

Proverbs 27:21

John 12:42-43

Matthew 5:16 (How does this instruction differ from the others? When is it acceptable to let your good works show?)

2. Heeding Parents' Advice

After suffering the consequences of not listening to her mother's advice, Katy says, "I do wonder if I shall ever really learn that mother knows more than I do!" (p. 6) This is a repeated theme throughout Katy's growing-up years. How could Katy have avoided these unpleasant consequences had she heeded the advice contained in the following Proverbs?

Proverbs 1:8

Proverbs 4:10

Proverbs 8:32-33

Proverbs 13:1

Proverbs 19:20

Proverbs 22:17

Proverbs 23:19

3. Jealousy

Why did Katy's purposeful self-denial (p. 9-10) not draw her closer to God? What does each of the following verses say about jealousy?

Romans 13:13

1 Corinthians 3:3

2 Corinthians 12:20

Galatians 5:19-23

4. Feelings vs. Facts

Katy doubts her love for God because of an absence of feelings. In other words, she cannot see her love for God as a part of her experience. What does Dr. Cabot say is the true test of whether or not we love God? (pp. 14-15) How does John 14:21 confirm that this is fact?

2 Corinthians 5:7 tells us that "*we walk by faith, not by sight*." Read Watchman Nee's story and commentary on this verse:

Fact, Faith, and Experience were walking along the top of a wall. Fact walked steadily on, turning neither to right nor left and never looking behind. Faith followed, and all went well so long as he kept his eyes focused upon Fact; but as soon as he became concerned about Experience and turned to see how *he* was getting on, he lost his balance and tumbled off the wall, and poor old Experience fell down after him.

All temptation is primarily to look within; to take our eyes off the Lord and to take account of appearances. Faith is always meeting a mountain, a mountain of evidence that seems to contradict God's Word, a mountain of apparent contradiction in the realm of tangible fact – of failures in deed, as well as in the realm of feeling and suggestion – and either faith or the mountain has to go. They cannot both stand. But the trouble is that many a time the mountain stays and faith goes. That must not be. If we resort to our senses to discover truth, we shall find Satan's lies are often enough true to our experience; but if we refuse to accept as binding anything that contradicts God's Word and maintain an attitude of faith in Him alone, we shall find instead that Satan's lies begin to dissolve and that *our experience is coming progressively to tally with that Word.* (59-60)

In the coming weeks we shall see Katy slowly but surely learning this lesson.

5. Ministry to the Grieving

Katy is amazed at her mother's behavior through the early stages of her grief when she loses her husband. "She seems to live in heaven," (p. 22) Katy remarks. She is particularly disgusted with silly, insensitive visitors. I am convinced that learning the delicate art of ministering to the grieving comes mostly through being ministered to by mature people during our own times of grief and through years of practice, but Scripture gives us some guidance in this area. Look up the following verses and comment.

2 Corinthians 1:3-4

Philippians 2:1-4

Romans 12:15

The Bible Emphasis: God's Answer to the Sin Dilemma

"If anybody but Mother had said that, my heart would have melted at once, and I would have gone right down to Dr. Cabot to be molded in his hands to almost any shape. But as it was I brushed past her, ran into my room, and locked my door. Oh, what makes me act so! I hate myself for it, I don't want to do it!" (p. 16)

Perhaps the words of our fictitious Katy Mortimer ring familiar of the words the apostle Paul penned almost 2000 years ago: *For that which I do I allow not: for what I would, that do I not; but what I hate, that do I.*" (Romans 7:15) (How is your memory work coming on this verse? Or have you selected another?)

The source of this dilemma and our way out of it comprise the subject of our Bible Emphasis this week. We will look at three power-packed chapters from the book of Romans, the most complete doctrinal treatise of the Gospel in all the Bible. Since we will merely be skimming the surface of the riches contained in these chapters, let me highlight the main theme we want to take from each:

A. THE TRUTH (FACT) OF OUR POSITION IN CHRIST (Romans Six)
B. WHY WE CONTINUE TO BATTLE DESPITE THE ABOVE TRUTH (Romans Seven)
C. HOW TO APPLY THE ROMANS SIX TRUTH TO WIN THE ROMANS SEVEN BATTLE
    (Romans Eight - the first 17 verses)

A. Read Romans 6.

    List the FACTS you learn about Christ in each of the following verses.

    Romans 6:4

    Romans 6:9

    Romans 6:10

    Romans 6:23

    List the FACTS you learn about yourself as a believer in each of the following verses:

Romans 6: 2

Romans 6:3

Romans 6:4

Romans 6:5

Romans 6:6

Romans 6:8

Romans 6:14

Romans 6:16

Romans 6:17

Romans 6:18

Romans 6:19a

Romans 6:20

Romans 6:22

The doctrine you have just examined is sometimes called "Our Union with Christ." It is the FACT that Katy by FAITH must stay focused on because it is the only sure basis for fighting sin.

Some Christians see the process of becoming Christ-like a simple matter of "Letting go and letting God." As Katy said of Amelia: "She says it is so easy to be a Christian!" (p. 17)

Note Paul's commands in the following verses and comment on this "let go – let God" perspective:

Romans 6:11

Romans 6:12

Romans 6:13

Romans 6:19

Surrendering everything we are and have to God as we come into union with Him is surely crucial to living an abundant life in Christ, but let us be sure that we understand the aggressive nature of the commands we are given to be ruthless with the sin we see in our own lives. We are in a war, dear ones! This war is against our own flesh that we love so much. Let's move on now to see why we still battle with sin despite our union with Christ.

B. Read Romans 7.

What is the point of Paul's illustration in Romans 7:1-3?

How does Romans 7:4-6 restate the doctrine that we examined in Romans 6? In these verses Paul adds the purpose for our union with Christ. What is it?

How does Romans 7:7-12 explain why Katy might have struggled with sin more than some girls from other families?

Do you find that the more you know of God's requirements, the more you realize how far short you fall? What then does Paul say is the purpose of the law? (Romans 7:7-8, 7:13)

Paul describes his frustrations with the flesh (the sinful nature) vividly in Romans 7:14-20. Can you relate? Why do we keep sinning even though we desire to please God? (Romans 7:21-23)

Katy's dilemma then – and Paul's – and ours as well – is that the flesh is still alive and well, and we often choose to give in to it. Where then lies our hope? Let's move on to Romans 8 for the answer.

C. Read Romans 8:1-17.

Why is there no condemnation for us who are in Christ? (Romans 8:2)

How did Christ meet the requirements of the law that we could never meet ourselves? (Romans 8:3-4)

Contrast life in the flesh to life in the Spirit on the chart below.

Life in the Flesh	Life in the Spirit
Romans 8: 5 -	Romans 8:5 -
Romans 8:6 -	Romans 8:6 -
Romans 8:7 -	
Romans 8:8 -	

List FACTS about yourself if the Spirit of God lives in you.

Romans 8:9

Romans 8:10

Romans 8:11

What must be our response to the FACTS in the above verses? (See Romans 8:13)

Add this aggressive command to those we read in Romans 6:11,12,13, and 19. Then come back to the marvelous FACTS about yourself in Romans 8:14-17. List those FACTS below.

Thank your Abba for these marvelous gifts from His hand and commit your lives to living in the light of Truth!

Personal Applications

1. The first application question will be the same each week. Here it is:
    Select ONE of the "Treasures from the Story." (This week there are five to choose from. See pp. 7-9 of the lesson.) You will want to select one through which God spoke personally to you.

    - If His message brought an eye-opening truth that comforted or encouraged you (We call this a promise), respond with gratitude.

    - If His message convicted you of sin, respond with confession and accept His forgiveness.

    - If His message instructed you to take some action (We call this a command), respond with obedience.

    Record His word to you and your response in your journal.

2. The second application question each week will pertain specifically to "The Bible Emphasis." Here is this week's question:

    Which FACT that we studied in Romans 6-8 means the most to you personally? Why? How will you respond to what you have learned? Record your answers in your journal.

Katy Deals with Worldliness

"The scanty, noisy, thirsty-producing streams of worldly delight only increase the feverish desires of the soul; but the tide of joy which flows in upon the Christian, is silent, deep, full and satisfying." (Payson 74)

Katy Deals with Worldliness

Love not the world, neither the things that are in the world. If any man love the world, the love of the Father is not in him. For all that is in the world, the lust of the flesh, and the lust of the eyes, and the pride of life, is not of the Father, but is of the world. And the world passeth away, and the lust thereof: but he that doeth the will of God abideth for ever.

1 John 2:15-17

Treasures from the Story

1. Our Deceitful Hearts

Jeremiah 17:9 tells us that ***"The heart is deceitful above all things, and desperately wicked: who can know it?"*** We see several examples of this truth in Katy's reactions to life in this week's reading.

Explain how each of the following situations verifies the truth of Jeremiah's words:

a. "Oh, if he (her father) had only had a sickness that needed our tender nursing, instead of being snatched from us in that sudden way!" (p. 26)

b. "Then I prayed - yes, I am sure I really prayed as I had not done for more than a year, and the idea of self-sacrifice grew every moment more beautiful in my eyes, till at last I felt an almost joyful triumph in writing to poor Charley, and telling him what I had resolved to do." (pp. 33-34)

c. "I have made up my mind never to tell a human soul about this affair. It will be so high-minded and honorable to shield him from the contempt he deserves. With all my faults I am glad that there is nothing mean or petty about me!" (p. 36)

d. "If I were a minister I am sure I would get my sermons done early in the week." (p. 40)

e. "Look at the dear little thing, Mother!" I cried; "doesn't she look like a line of poetry?" (p. 55)

2. Portrait of a Godly Mother

Katy's portrayal of her mother provides a beautiful example of a godly woman for us to follow. Match the quotations in the left column below with the Scriptures in the right column describing the character qualities exemplified.

"If what you say of Amelia is true, it is most ungenerous of you to tell of it. But I do not believe it. Amelia Gordon has too much good sense to be carried away by a handsome face and agreeable manners." (p. 28) Scripture: _____

" Oh, my poor child, how my selfish sorrow has made me neglect you." (p. 28) Scripture: _____

"Mother shut herself up, and I have no doubt prayed over it. I really believe she prays over every new dress she buys." (p. 29) Scripture: _____

"At last she said she would put us on one year's probation. Charley might spend one evening here . . . consent to our engagement." (p. 29) Scripture: _____

"I wonder if mother knew it (that Charley had money) when she opposed our engagement so strenuously. I have asked her, and she said she did." (p. 37) Scripture: _____

Philippians 2:3-4
Let *nothing* be done *through strife or vainglory; but in lowliness of mind let each esteem other better than themselves. Look not every man on his own things, but every man also on the things of others.*

1 Corinthians 13:6-7
(Charity) Rejoiceth not in iniquity, but rejoiceth in the truth; Beareth all things, believeth all things, hopeth all things, endureth all things.

Proverbs 31:26
She openeth her mouth with wisdom; and in her tongue is the law of kindness.

Titus 2:11-14
For the grace of God that bringeth salvation hath appeared to all men, Teaching us that, denying ungodliness and worldly lusts, we should live soberly, righteously, and godly, in this present world; Looking for that blessed hope, and the glorious appearing of the great God and our Saviour Jesus Christ; Who gave himself for us, that he might redeem us from all iniquity, and purify unto himself a peculiar people, zealous of good works.

James 1:5
If any of you lack wisdom, let him ask of God, that giveth to all men liberally, and upbraideth not; and it shall be given him.

3. Believing the Facts

How and why did peace finally come to Katy? (pp. 39-40)

The following verses are just a few examples of the kind of verses Katy needed to copy in her journal or write on note cards to carry with her, meditate on, and memorize. *("We have thought of thy lovingkindness, O God, in the midst of thy temple."* - Psalm 48:9) In developing this discipline, she would have the tool she needed to combat the enemy when he whispered his lie into her ear that she could never be good enough to be accepted by God. Look up these verses and notice the prevailing theme of them all. What does each one say about God's love?

Psalm 44:3

Isaiah 54:10

Romans 5:8

Romans 8:38-39

Are you beginning to develop this discipline? Have you written your memory verse for the week into your journal and are you meditating on it and memorizing it? Or have you written any other verses that God is using in your life into your journal or on note cards to meditate upon and memorize?

4. Responding to the Facts

What evidence of a changed life emerges almost immediately in Katy's behavior when she begins to believe the FACT that she is *"accepted in the beloved"*? (Ephesians 1:6) (p. 40)

Read the following verses and note several responses to God's love that are to be evident in His children.

Psalm 89:1-2

Psalm 107:21

John 13:34-35

John 15:9-10

1 John 3:16-18

5. Trustworthiness in Small Matters

Katy does not see the change that occurs in her once she accepts the fact that God loves her; and after several acts of kindness, she remarks, "But I could not think of anything to do for God. I wish I could." (p. 40) Later Mrs. Cabot helps her change her perspective on her desire to "perform some truly noble, self-sacrificing acts." (p. 45) What is her advice to Katy on pages 46-47? How does Mrs. Cabot recognize the truth of the parable in Luke 19:11-26? (Particularly note verse 17.)

The Bible Emphasis: Worldliness

Katy reveals a glimpse of her worldly tastes when she speaks of borrowing all the latest novels from Jenny. (p. 25) Later she says that she "got frightened at my novel reading propensities, and resolved not to look into one for twelve months. . . . Now I hope and believe that the back of this dangerous taste is broken, and that I shall never be *a slave to it* again." (p. 42) Oh, that we as 21st century Christian women would "get frightened" at our propensity toward the things of this world as our young heroine did!

Let's take a look at the subject of worldliness in Scripture. What does the word *world* mean in the Bible? What happened to this world after creation? Why are there so many warnings to Christians about the temptations of the world? As Christians, how can we keep from being worldly?

The Greek word *kosmos* used in the New Testament means by derivation "the ordered world." The following verses reveal that God is the origin of this ordered world, or what we sometimes call "the universe."

> **God that made the <u>world</u> and all things therein, seeing that he is Lord of heaven and earth, dwelleth not in temples made with hands;** (Acts 17:24)

> *He (Jesus) was in the world,* **and the <u>world</u> was made by him,** *and the world knew him not.* (John 1:10)

Because mankind is the most important part of the universe, the word *kosmos* is more often used in Scripture for human beings. It is this world to which John refers in John 3:16.

> ***For God so loved the <u>world</u>, that he gave his only begotten Son, that whosoever believeth in him should not perish, but have everlasting life.*** (John 3:16)

We know from studying the Bible that this world of human beings, the climax of divine creation, the world that God made especially to reflect His glory, is now in rebellion against Him. Through the transgression of Adam, sin entered into it with universal consequences (Romans 5:18). It has become, as a result, a ***disordered*** world. (***New Bible Dictionary*** 1261)

Read the following verses to see who now controls this fallen world and has the authority to present to us all the world has to offer. What price must we pay for these things of the world?

1 John 5:19

Matthew 4:8-10

Because of these sad facts, the word ***world*** in the New Testament frequently has sinister significance. It no longer signifies the creation that God intended it to be, but instead signifies the kingdom set against God, following its own wisdom and living by the light of its own reason, not recognizing the Source of all true life and illumination. (***New Bible Dictionary*** 1261)

Notice this use of the word ***world*** in the following verses:

1 Corinthians 1:21

John 1:10

The New Bible Dictionary defines ***worldliness*** as "the enthronement of something other than God as the supreme object of man's interests and affections. Pleasures and occupations, not necessarily wrong in themselves, become so when an all-absorbing attention is paid to them." (New Bible Dictionary 1261)

Read Mark 4:3-8; 13-20 (Focus on the 3rd seed of this parable: verses 7 and 18-19.) List on the chart on the next page the three things (thorns) that cause a person not to bear fruit. Explain how these thorns relate to the above definition of worldliness. Give an example of each of these three potential thorns in your own life that could keep you from bearing fruit for the Kingdom of God.

	What it is	How it relates to worldliness	An example of it in your own life
Thorn #1			
Thorn #2			
Thorn #3			

Some teachers interpret the people represented by the third seed as unsaved; others interpret them as worldly Christians. Let's explore in more depth what God's Word says about each of these three thorns. Then, on the basis of your discoveries, you can decide which interpretation you will embrace.

Thorn #1: The Cares of This World

Read Luke 14:15-24. What kinds of life cares did the people in this parable have that kept them from coming to the great banquet? What was the result for them? How can you relate to these cares?

Read Matthew 6:25-33. How does Jesus instruct us to think about the cares of this world?

Thorn #2: The Deceitfulness of Riches

Read Luke 12:13-21. How was the man in this parable deceived by riches?

Can you think of some examples where we may deceive ourselves about the things of the world and try to spiritualize our covetousness?

What is the fate of a man who is deceived by riches, according to the following verses?

Psalm 49:16-20

Proverbs 14:12

The deceitfulness of riches can make us complacent about the needs around us. Read these sobering words of the prophet Amos spoken to Israel before they went into exile for their rebellion. How are these words instructive to the American church of the 21st century? To you?

Amos 6:3-7

Warren Wiersbe makes the following observations on these verses:

> **Amos leveled his attack at those living in complacency and luxury in both Israel and Judah. Great wealth and comfortable life-styles may make people think they are secure, but God is not pleased if we isolate ourselves from others' needs. God wants us to care for others as he cares for us. His kingdom has no place for selfishness or indifference. We must learn to put the needs of others before our wants. Using our wealth to help others is one way to guard against pride and complacency.** ("Be" Series)

In 1 Corinthians 7:29-31, Paul explains how we are to use the gifts that God has given us while we are on earth. What reason does he give for having such a perspective? How will this perspective keep us from complacency about the temporal abundance God has given us?

Thorn #3: The Lusts of Other Things

Read 1 John 2:15-17. How does this third thorn relate to the deceitfulness of riches?

Read these Old Testament warnings about allowing the lusts of other things to control you.

Micah 6:14

Haggai 1:5-6

Years before the prophets Micah and Haggai warned Israel of the consequences of idolatry (worldliness), the famous King Solomon had already given testimony to the meaninglessness of trying to find lasting satisfaction in anything or anyone but God Himself. Read this moving testimony from the wisest man who ever lived, and note some of the "lusts of other things" that he pursued in addition to riches.

Ecclesiastes 2:1-12

How then can we overcome these thorns so that we become fruit bearers? The answer lies at the center of the Gospel message. Christ freed men from the world's sinister forces by Himself engaging in mortal combat with the devil, who continually instigates evil within the world. By voluntarily submitting to death, Jesus defeated the devil. On the cross, judgment was passed on the "ruler of this world." Faith in Christ as the Son of God whose sacrifice alone can cleanse men from guilt and the power of sin enables the believer to overcome the world. (New Bible Dictionary 1261)

> *For whatsoever is born of God overcometh the world: and this is the victory that overcometh the world, even our faith. [5]Who is he that overcometh the world, but he that believeth that Jesus is the Son of God?* (1 John 5:4-5)

We are in bondage to the spirit of this world which controls human reason and understanding until Christ frees us. Only a true knowledge of God as revealed by Christ can prevent us from totally rejecting truth or from pretending to be spiritual when, in fact, we are worldly to the core.

Read Jesus' prayer for his disciples shortly before His death in John 17:6-19. As followers of Christ, how are we related to the world?

What will protect us from the evil one? (See John 17:11,17)

Paul counsels us on how to train our minds away from the seductions of this world and towards the truth (FACTS) that Jesus says sanctifies us. Note his advice in each of the following verses.

Romans 12:2

Philippians 3:18-19

Colossians 3:2-5

May God help us to be **in** the world, giving life and hope to the dead and hopeless, but not **of** the world, conforming to its mold!

Personal Applications

(Remember to record your responses to these two questions in your journal.)

1. Select ONE of the "Treasures from the Story." (See pp. 17-20 of the lesson.) You will want to select one through which God spoke personally to you.

   - If His message brought an eye-opening truth that comforted or encouraged you (We call this a promise), respond with gratitude.

   - If His message convicted you of sin, respond with confession and accept His forgiveness.

   - If His message instructed you to take some action (We call this a command), respond with obedience.

2. Which thorn from the parable of the sower do you find most frequently chokes out the Word in your life, making it unfruitful? What practical steps can you take to rid your soil of this thorn?

Katy Grows in God's Word

Pliable speaking to Christian about the Bible:
   "And do you think that the words of your book are certainly true?"
   "Yes, verily, for it was made by Him that cannot lie." (Bunyan 5-6)

Katy Grows in God's Word

All scripture is given by inspiration of God, and is profitable for doctrine, for reproof, for correction, for instruction in righteousness: That the man of God may be perfect, thoroughly furnished unto all good works. 2 Timothy 3:16-17

Treasures from the Story

1. A Mother's Wisdom

I simply love Katy's mother and long for the godly wisdom she displays in relating to her 20 year old daughter. When Katy calls Susan Green "that dirty old woman!" (p. 56), Mother holds her tongue, exhibiting a degree of self-control that is the fruit of God's Holy Spirit. How is Mother revealing that she truly believes Philippians 1:6 for Katy?

As the discussion continues, how does Mother respond wisely, and again supernaturally? (p. 56)

How can we apply Mother's example to raising our children as well as to edifying our Christian friends and acquaintances who are not growing spiritually as fast as WE think they should? See 1 Thessalonians 5:14-15.

2. Lessons from a Deathbed

Susan Green's death traumatizes Katy in a different way from the death of her father. Seeing the fleeting nature of this life brings her face to face with two ugly observations about her own heart:

Observation One:

"I remembered what I had once said to Mrs. Cabot about having tasteful things about me, with a sort of shudder. What a mockery they are in the awful presence of death!" (p. 59)

How is Katy learning the truth of 1 Timothy 6:17-19, written by the apostle Paul to a young pastor?

Paul had learned this truth from the Master Himself. How does Jesus address this truth in Matthew 6:19-21?

Observation Two:

"I would have felt myself quite a heroine . . . if I had not been overcome with bitter regret that I had not, with firmness and dignity, turned poor Susan's last thoughts to her Savior. Oh, how could I, through miserable cowardice, let those precious moments slip by!" (pp. 59-60)

In a second letter to the same young pastor Timothy, Paul exhorts him to be bold in his witness. Read 2 Timothy 1:1-9 and record what you learn.

Even Paul himself feels the need for prayer support over the issue of boldness. Read Ephesians 6:19-20. Why might Katy make the same prayer request?

3. Dr. Cabot's Lessons

Dr. Cabot's letter to Katy is filled with godly counsel and wisdom. Below are several of his quotations. Look up the Scripture reference that accompanies each and write it out in the space provided. Then try to summarize the principle or command that is the FACT Dr. Cabot is emphasizing. The first two have been done for you.

a. "Now He never leaves His work incomplete, and He will gradually lead you into clear and open vision, if you will allow Him to do it." (p. 61)

   Philippians 1:6: *"Being confident of this very thing, that he which hath begun a good work in you will perform it until the day of Jesus Christ."*

   FACT: *God always finishes the work He begins in us at salvation.*

b. ". . . and he was restored, and saw every man clearly. . . . in order to have it done (for you) you must go to Christ Himself, not to one of His servants." (p. 61)

   James 1:5: *"If any of you lack wisdom, let him ask of God, that giveth to all men liberally, and upbraideth not; and it shall be given him."*

   FACT: *For clear spiritual vision, we must go to Christ Himself, not to people, even godly ones.*

c. "Having been pardoned by your God and Savior, the next thing you have to do is to show
your gratitude for this infinite favor by consecrating yourself entirely to Him, body, soul,
and spirit. . . .He has bought you with a price, and you are no longer your own. . . . He
asks, and He has a right to ask, for all you have and all you are." (p. 62)

1 Corinthians 6:19-20: _____

_____

FACT: _____

_____

d. "Remember that it is His *will* that you should be sanctified, and that the work of making
you holy is His, not yours. At the same time you are not to sit with folded hands, waiting
for this blessing. You are to avoid laying hindrances in His way, and you are to exercise
faith in Him . . ." (pp. 62-63)

Isaiah 26:12: _____

_____

FACT: _____

_____

e. ". . . and if you have real faith in Him you will not insist on knowing this reason. If you
find, in the course of daily events, . . . that your will revolts at His will – do not be
discouraged, but fly to your Savior and stay in His presence . . every such consent to
suffer will bring you nearer and nearer to Him; and in this nearness to Him you will find
such peace . . ." (p. 63)

Matthew 26:42: _____

_____

FACT: _____

_____

f. "You can will to choose for your associates those who are most devout and holy." (p. 63)

Psalm 1:1: _____

_____

FACT: _____

_____

g. "You can will to read books that will stimulate you in your Christian life, rather than those that merely amuse." (p. 64) (Add to this thought: " . . . read magazines, watch movies, videos, or TV")

Philippians 4:8: _____

_____

FACT: _____

_____

h. "You can will to prefer a religion of principle to one of mere feeling; in other words, to obey the will of God when no comfortable glow of emotion accompanies your obedience." (p. 64)

1 Corinthians 9:27: _____

_____

FACT: _____

_____

4. Using Our Talents

Where does Katy's confusion lie about using her talents? (pp. 66-68) What light do the following verses shed on her confusion?

Colossians 3:23

1 Corinthians 10:31

1 Peter 4:11

Mother offers Katy wise counsel on pages 67-68 concerning the use of our talents. Practically speaking, in your own life, how can you enjoy the recreation that Mother claims "we must have" while at the same time applying the truth of the above three verses? Can you relate to Katy's lament: ". . . the more I delight in them (her music and drawing), the less I delight in God"? (p. 68) What progress are you making toward a solution to this dilemma?

5. Dorcas

Read about Dorcas in Acts 9:36-42 if you are not familiar with Katy's allusion to her on p. 78. Katy is specifically referring to Acts 9:36. Who was Dorcas and for what is she remembered? (Explanation is also given in the footnote of the text.)

The Bible Emphasis: The Word of God

Katy's family members have obviously built their lives and homes on the Word of God. Throughout her journal, Katy frequently alludes to specific Bible texts as she is recording a thought or happening. For our Bible Emphasis this week, let's take a look at what God's Word has to say about itself.

Read 2 Peter 1:20-21. Who wrote the Bible according to Peter?

Read 2 Timothy 2:15. How are we to approach the Bible?

Read 2 Timothy 3:16-17

How does this verse confirm Peter's statement above? How is the Bible useful to us? List the four ways on the chart on the next page.

Ways the Bible is useful to us	Greek word	Definition
1.	*didaskalia*	Instruction, doctrine, learning, teaching. Refers also to the authority of the teacher behind the teaching
2.	*elegchos*	Proof, conviction, evidence; the acknowledgement of the truth of the accusation on the part of the accused, i.e. confession
3.	*epanorthosis*	Literally, a straightening up; reformation; correction or amendment of what is wrong in a man's life; restoration to an upright state; improvement of life and character
4.	*paideia*	Originally meant the instruction of a child; education or training; instruction, nurture; by implication, disciplinary correction or chastening

(Zodhiates 896, 902, 904, 926, and Vine 233, 324)

As you study the definitions of these four words, turn back to the instructions you have followed in the first two lessons under Question #1 of "Personal Applications." Notice that we have already assumed that when God speaks to us through His Word, His message will be profitable to our lives in various ways.

First, it will be profitable for teaching us basic biblical beliefs. The word ***doctrine*** frightens some, but all of the FACTS that we have been delighting in as we have begun this Bible study (God loves us; We have been set free from sin by Christ's death and resurrection; Jesus has overcome the world, etc.) are Christian doctrine. The word simply refers a set of beliefs. If you have responded with gratitude to an eye-opening truth that has comforted or encouraged you - a promise from God to you – you have found the Scriptures "profitable for doctrine."

Secondly, God's Word will be profitable for convicting us of sin in our lives, not only to bring us to saving faith, but continually throughout our Christian lives, as we submit to His reproof. If you have responded with sorrow and confession to a convicting Word from Him, you have found the Scriptures profitable "for reproof."

Thirdly, once God's Word shows us the error of our ways, it will also show us how to correct those ways. Our third word contains the root word *orthos* in the Greek, which you may recognize as a root that is often used in English to speak of straightening, as in *orthopedics*.

Both our third and our fourth words refer to the third step we have looked at each week in our "Personal Applications." As we walk with Christ, His Holy Spirit is our Teacher, our Trainer. He is educating us to become like Him with correction and instruction, as well as with nurture. If you have responded to an instruction from Him (a command) with a step of obedience, you have found the Scriptures profitable "for correction, for instruction in righteousness."

Turn now to Psalm 119. This psalm is an acrostic poem. Each stanza takes one letter of the Hebrew alphabet and uses that letter to begin each verse of that stanza. This technique is, of course, impossible to detect in the English translation, but it explains why the Psalm is so long!

Look through the Psalm and find at least ten words that describe God's Word. List them below along with the verse.

1. _____   5. _____   8. _____

2. _____   6. _____   9. _____

3. _____   7. _____   10. _____

4. _____

Now find at least five things that God's Word does. List them below along with the verse.

1. _____   4. _____

2. _____   5. _____

3. _____

May we as women of God be "thoroughly furnished unto all good works" as we learn to love the Word of God the way the Psalmist does!

Personal Applications

(Remember to record your responses to these two questions in your journal.)

1. Select ONE of the "Treasures from the Story." (See pp. 29-33 of the lesson.)

    *   If God's message brought an eye-opening truth that comforted or encouraged you (We call this a promise), respond with gratitude. (DOCTRINE)

    *   If His message convicted you of sin, respond with confession and accept His forgiveness. (REPROOF)

    *   If His message instructed you to take some action (We call this a command), respond with obedience. (CORRECTION AND INSTRUCTION IN RIGHTEOUSNESS)

2. What new truth did you learn about the Word of God that will change the way you approach your Bible study?

Lesson Four
(Chapters 9-10: pp. 83-106)

Katy's Disappointment

"Go and tell Jesus; well He knows
   The human heart; its pangs, its throes;
He will not fail Thee, He will be
   Friend, Comforter, and Peace to thee." (Prentiss 66)

Katy's Disappointment

They cried unto thee, and were delivered: they trusted in thee, and were not confounded. (or disappointed) Psalm 22:5

(Have you been memorizing Scripture each week? Be sure to go back and review.)

Treasures from the Story

1. Humility

Why does Katy's mother call her a "contrary child" (p. 89) for not accepting her praise? Isn't Katy just being humble?

What is true humility, according to God? In searching for answers to this question, I was stunned to discover that God the Father Himself embodies this virtue. Although I had clearly understood the humility of God the Son in emptying Himself and coming to earth as a man to die, I had never noticed that the God of Israel demonstrated humility to His Old Testament servants! Look at this:

David sang to the Lord the words recorded in Psalm 18 after the Lord had delivered him from the hand of all his enemies and from the hand of Saul.

Read Psalm 18:1-7 to get the context. Then focus on verse 35. Your translation may read "stoop down" or "gentleness." The Hebrew word is `*anavah*, meaning "condescension, modesty, gentleness, humility, meekness." (Strong 90)

Now read Psalm 113:5-9. (The same Hebrew word describes God here in verse 6.) What does God's humility look like in these passages?

The magnificent New Testament example of humility, of course, is that of our Lord Jesus. Read Philippians 2:5-8. What characterizes Christ's humility?

Read John 13:2-5. Note specifically the basis from which Jesus was able to humble Himself to perform this lowly task for His apostles.

Read the following verses. What virtue apparently accompanies humility?

Proverbs 11:2

Proverbs 15:33

James 3:13

Read the following verses to see God's rewards for humility.

Psalm 147:6

Psalm 149:4

1 Peter 5:5

Proverbs 27:21 tells us: *"As the fining pot for silver, and the furnace for gold; so is a man to his praise."* What does this mean? How does it relate to Katy? To you?

2. The Tongue

When Katy compliments Dr. Elliott on his gentle touch to his burn victim, he responds: "I am glad you begin to find that even stones feel, sometimes." (p. 94) If you have forgotten Katy's earlier unkind words to him, review page 74. Notice the wound that Dr. Elliott still carries, months later, from those careless words. Study the following Scriptures for wise advice on the tongue:

Job 16:5

Proverbs 12:18

Proverbs 15:1-2, 4, 32

Proverbs 16:21; 23-24

Proverbs 17:27-28

Proverbs 18:21

Proverbs 21:19

Proverbs 24:29

Proverbs 31:26

Ephesians 4:26,29

Colossians 4:6

3. The Heart Connection to the Tongue

Katy further blunders with her tongue when she blurts out in the midst of an argument with Dr. Elliott: "I have to say what I think." Dr. E. replies: "It is well to think rightly, then." (p. 94) How does he understand Jesus' words of Matthew 15:17-20?

4. The Sin Dilemma Reviewed

How does Katy's little drama on pp. 95-96 relate to our study in Romans 7 the first week? What is the correct answer to Katy's question at the end of Chapter 9? "Am I Katy or am I Kate?" (p. 96)

5. Differences in Men and Women

In Katy's description of her first month of marriage to Ernest (pp. 100-101), I find deep insights into the differences between men and women. (And this was a century before Dobson, Trent, Smalley, and Chapman gave us all their wisdom on gender differences, love languages, and the like!) Note some of the differences that create conflict between husbands and wives which are revealed in this scene. Apply any biblical principles you have learned on marriage in your past studies to your observations.

The Bible Emphasis: Disappointment

Webster defines **disappoint** as "to defeat of expectation or hope; to fail to come up to the expectation of." Our story characters deal with a variety of disappointments in this section of our story. Name a few of them.

Dr. Elliott, after his bitter disappointment of being spurned by Katy, turns his pain into an edifying message that Katy says he spoke "cheerfully and hopefully." (p. 90)

List the three areas that will disappoint us, according to Dr. Elliott. (p. 90):

1.

2.

3.

Let us examine what God's Word says about each of these three areas of disappointment.

Disappointment #1: SELF

Romans 7:7-25: Review, if necessary. (You may not even have to peek there by now to be able to answer how this passage relates to Dr. E's first category of disappointment!) From what you know of Paul's internal struggle, what is the solution to his disappointment with himself? You may have to sneak a peek at Romans 8:1-2 if you have forgotten his answer.

Disappointment #2: FRIENDS (and other people)

Job 6:14-21: In whom is Job disappointed? Why?

Job 42:7-16: What is the solution to his disappointment?
(If you are not familiar with the story of Job, these short passages may be confusing. We will discuss the context in class.)

Psalm 41:7-13 and Psalm 55:12-23: In whom is David disappointed? What is his solution?

2 Timothy 4:9-10; 16-17: In whom is Paul disappointed? What is his solution?

Disappointment #3: THE WORLD (and the circumstances of life)

Read Jeremiah 2:1-9. How have the Israelites disappointed God?

Read Jeremiah 2:13, 18. What illustration does God use in these two verses to describe the sins of His people? (If you don't know how a cistern is used, find out.)

Read Jeremiah 2:36-37. What does God warn His people that they will be disappointed in?

What is the obvious solution to the disappointment they will experience because of their waywardness?

Read the following passages for further confirmation of the only place to turn where we will not be disappointed.

Psalm 22:2-5

Isaiah 49:22-23

Romans 5:1-5

If we live very long, times will surely come when we experience (feel) disappointment with God Himself. Go back to Lesson One and review Watchman Nee's story on page 9 of our Bible Study. What we are to do when EXPERIENCE does not line up with the FACTS in God's Word?

Read Jeremiah's words in Lamentations 3:1-26. How does he handle the crisis of being disappointed with God? How can you follow Jeremiah's example?

Personal Applications

(Remember to record your responses to these two questions in your journal.)

1. Select ONE of the "Treasures from the Story." (See pp. 39-41 of the lesson.)

   - If God's message brought an eye-opening truth that comforted or encouraged you (We call this a promise), respond with gratitude. (DOCTRINE)

   - If His message convicted you of sin, respond with confession and accept His forgiveness. (REPROOF)

   - If His message instructed you to take some action (We call this a command), respond with obedience. (CORRECTION AND INSTRUCTION IN RIGHTEOUSNESS)

2. Which of the three areas of disappointment did you relate to the most and why? Ask God to give you the peace and contentment that comes from knowing that He will never disappoint you and that He is the true Satisfier.

Katy Learns the Value of Suffering

"It is good, too, that we sometimes suffer opposition, and that men think ill of us and misjudge us, even when we do and mean well. Such things are an aid to humility, and preserve us from pride and vainglory. For we more readily turn to God as our inward witness, when men despise us and think no good of us."
(Thomas a Kempis 39)

Katy Learns the Value of Suffering

Wherein (your spiritual birth) *ye greatly rejoice, though now for a season, if need be, ye are in heaviness through manifold temptations: That the trial of your faith, being much more precious than of gold that perisheth, though it be tried with fire, might be found unto praise and honour and glory at the appearing of Jesus Christ: 1 Peter 1:6-7*

Treasures from the Story

1. Respecting Our Husbands

"If I could have told my troubles to someone I could thus have found vent for them; but there was no one to whom I had a right to speak of my husband." (p. 108)

How quickly Katy is maturing into a godly woman! As Christian wives, we sometimes chaff at the instruction in Ephesians 5:22:

> **"Wives, submit yourselves unto your own husbands, as unto the Lord."**

My husband claims that even Christian husbands who are biblically illiterate know two verses of Scripture: John 3:16 and Ephesians 5:22! The passage beginning with the instruction to submit closes, however, with a verse that is perhaps even more significant for us wives to meditate on:

> **. . . and the wife see that she reverence her husband.** (Ephesians 5:33b)

How is Katy showing reverence by not "venting" her troubles to others? Have you ever spoken of your husband to another person in a way that dishonored him? Is it ever right to discuss your husband's shortcomings with another person?

2. Making Our Words Match Our Actions

Look up the following Scriptures and apply them to Ernest's remark: "Speaking beautifully is little to the purpose unless one lives beautifully." (p. 109)

Isaiah 29:13

Mark 7:6

1 Corinthians 13:1

James 1:22

1 John 3:18

3. The Mind Battle

Katy says to Ernest, "I only want those little daily assurances of your affection which I should suppose would be spontaneous if you felt at all towards me as I do to you." (p. 109)

Notice in this statement that Katy is making a false assumption. The assumption is:

Daily affection from my husband would be spontaneous if he really loved me. (Call this Premise #1)

If Katy is going to practice Logic 101, here is where that false assumption must take her:

Daily affection from my husband is not spontaneous. (Call this Premise #2)

Therefore, my husband does not love me. (Call this the Conclusion)

When we begin with one false premise, even if the second premise is true, (and notice that it is), we will always end up with a false conclusion.

Here is another example of Katy's twisted logic (p. 115):

Premise #1: I thought you admired Martha and wanted me to be like her.

Premise #2: I can never be like Martha.

Conclusion: You will never esteem me as much as you do her.

How is Katy making the same mistake in her thinking in this example?

Now that we have identified the error in Katy's thinking, let's find the solution in Scripture. Read 2 Corinthians 10:3-5. What is Katy to do when she falls into the trap of entertaining false assumptions [vain imaginations (KJV)] in her mind?

The key to bringing into captivity every thought to the obedience of Christ rests in knowing the facts. Katy must be careful to learn the facts so that she will not be operating on the basis of lies.

In the first example, the fact that chased away her wrong conclusion, or lie, came from the mouth of Ernest: "I am absorbed in my work. It brings many grave cares and anxieties. I spend most of my time amid scenes of suffering and at dying beds. This makes me seem abstracted and cold, but it does not make you less dear. On the contrary, the sense it gives me of the brevity and sorrowfulness of life makes you doubly precious . . . . (p. 109)

In the second example, Ernest's words also revealed the fact that cast down the lie: "I admire her, but I do not want you to be like anybody but yourself." (p. 115)

Can you think of other examples where Katy misinterprets a situation, thus falling into the error warned against in the above verses? (Hint: See pp. 122-3, 129) What about you? When have you erred in this way?

Now let's look at the specific weapons with which we are to fight these mind battles, in addition to making sure that we have the facts of the situation. Read Ephesians 6:17-18.

What two weapons are specifically identified here that are mighty through God to the pulling down of strong holds?

As we use the strong weapon of the Word of God (THE FACTS) against the lies of Satan, praying for God to open our eyes to His Truth, we will begin to win our mind battles. This is an important concept which will surface again later in our study. If you do not choose to memorize the selected verse for this week, 2 Corinthians 10:3-5 would be an excellent choice. Better yet: begin to work on both of them!

4. Being Teachable

Katy persists in begging Ernest to be more demonstrative. His response is, "Then you must teach me." (p. 110) Go back to Ephesians 5:22 and look at the verse immediately before this one. How is Ernest carrying out this instruction in Ephesians 5:21 by inviting Katy to teach him to show his affections to her? Have you ever responded in this godly way when your husband asked you to act differently in some way?

5. Honoring Our Parents

Before Katy even realized that Ernest was God's choice for her husband, she had heard from Mrs. Embury that he was "the most devoted son she ever saw, and that he . . made such sacrifices for his parents." (p. 85) In theory, that sounded like a wonderful quality in a man. The reality for Katy, however, came to mean sacrifices on her part as well as his when Ernest assumes his father's debts.

Read the following Scriptures for a glimpse of God's Word on how we are to treat our parents.

Deuteronomy 5:16

Proverbs 17:6

Proverbs 17:25

Proverbs 20:20

Proverbs 23:22

Proverbs 23:24

Matthew 15:3-6

Luke 2:41-52

Ephesians 6:1-2

1 Timothy 5:4

In contrast to these instructions on honoring and obeying our parents, another side emerges in the Scriptures as well, from the lips of the Master Himself. Read these verses for a balance.

Matthew 19:5

Mark 10:29

Mark 13:12-13

Luke 8:19-21

Luke 9:59-60

Luke 14:26

Summarize what the Bible teaches on how we as adult Christians are to treat our parents.

6. Ernest Mirth

Ernest explains to Katy that his father "cannot understand that real earnestness and real, genuine mirthfulness are consistent with each other." (p. 116)

Read Nehemiah 8:1-12. The context for this narrative is that the Jews have returned to their homeland after 70 years of exile in Babylon for disobedience. Nehemiah has led them in rebuilding the walls of Jerusalem, and they are in the process of reestablishing a community that will honor God.

How do the people respond to hearing the Law?

How do their leaders instruct them to respond?

How are both responses good and right in the eyes of God, and what does this have to do with Katy's discussion with Father?

The Bible Emphasis: Suffering

"Oh, To Be Like Thee . . ." we sing to Jesus with gusto on Sunday mornings. But do we realize what we declare with those words? Read Isaiah 53 for a snapshot of the life of Jesus. According to this chapter of Scripture, what is involved in becoming like the Suffering Servant? (Isaiah 53:11)

Do you still want to be like Him, even if it means bearing His reproach?

Katy hears the same counsel from Mrs. Campbell that earlier she has read from her mother. Mother advised her to "constantly remind myself that my Heavenly Father has *chosen* to give me this care and trial (difficult people to live with) on the very threshold of my married life." (p. 110) Mrs. Campbell says, "If God chooses quite another lot for you (rather than a home full of congenial people), you may be sure that He sees that you need something totally different from what you want." (p. 125)

Katy responds to this thought with a question: "Was God really asking me not merely to let Martha and her father live with me on mere tolerance, but to rejoice that He had seen fit to let them harass and embitter my domestic life (p. 125)?"

In the coming weeks we will find Katy facing much deeper levels of suffering than living with difficult people; but let us take a look this week at what God's Word has to say about the subject of suffering.

Read the Scriptures below and record what you learn in each about suffering.

Psalm 119:67

Luke 13:1-5

Acts 5:40-42

2 Corinthians 4:5-12

2 Corinthians 12:7-10

Romans 5:1-5

Romans 8:17-18

Galatians 6:7-8

James 1:2-4

1 Peter 1:6-7

1 Peter 2:19-25

1 Peter 4:12-17

Summarize the teaching of Scripture on the subject of suffering from what you have studied.

Do you still want to be like Jesus, the Suffering Servant?

Personal Applications

(Remember to record your responses to these two questions in your journal.)

1. Select ONE of the "Treasures from the Story." (See pp. 47-52 of the lesson.)

   • If God's message brought an eye-opening truth that comforted or encouraged you, respond with gratitude. (DOCTRINE)

   • If His message convicted you of sin, respond with confession and accept His forgiveness. (REPROOF)

   • If His message instructed you to take some action, respond with obedience. (CORRECTION AND INSTRUCTION IN RIGHTEOUSNESS)

2. Andrew Murray writes specifically about the suffering that comes through dealing with difficult people:

   > **Let us look on every brother or sister who tries or vexes us as God's means of grace. Let us look on him or her as God's instrument for our purification, for our exercise of the humility Jesus, our life, breathes within us. And let us have such faith in the all of God and the nothing of self, that we may, in God's power, seek only to serve one another in love.** (Murray 50)

   Respond to this thought.

Katy's Faith

"Faith is an humble, self-denying grace; it makes the Christian nothing in himself and all in God." (Leighton 40)

Katy's Faith

Now faith is the substance of things hoped for, the evidence of things not seen. Hebrews 11:1

Treasures from the Story

1. The Mind Battle, Continued

Upon hearing Dr. Cabot refer to Ernest's financial struggles, Katy exclaims, "Instantly my idol was rudely thrown down from his pedestal. How *could* he reveal to Dr. Cabot a secret he had pretended it cost him so much to confide to me, his wife?" (p. 138) Note that this is January 30.

Almost a month later she writes, "Things have not gone on well of late. Dearly as I love Ernest, he has lowered himself in my eye by telling that to Dr. Cabot. . . . He is all shut up within himself . . . It must be that he is bitterly disappointed in me, and takes refuge in this awful silence." (p. 138)

On August 1, Ernest comes to see Katy while she is spending the summer with Mother. After three days of "nice long talks," what discovery does Katy make about her thinking concerning Ernest's talking to Dr. Cabot? (pp. 142-143) What further discovery does she make (p. 144) concerning Ernest's treatment of his sister Martha?

How has Katy fallen into the same sin we discussed in Lesson Five – "Treasures from the Story" - #3 (pp. 48-49 of our Bible Study). Review the solution to this sin found in 2 Corinthians 10:3-5.

Read Ephesians 4:25-27. How has Katy given "place to the devil" over the last six months?

2. Getting Away

At the end of Ernest's visit, Katy concludes, "After this all our cloud melted away. I only long to go home and show Ernest that he shall have one cheerful face about him, and have one cheerful voice." (p. 144) Read Jesus' words in Mark 6:31. How can you apply to a marriage relationship the invitation Jesus gives His disciples, as illustrated in Katy and Ernest's marriage?

3. Fear of Death

Father says to Katy, "I never saw (a death bed) where there was not some dread of the King of Terrors exhibited, nor one where there was such absolute *certainty* of having found favor with God .. ." (p. 149-150)

Read the following verses to discover on what basis we are able to overcome our fear of death.

Psalm 23:4

Isaiah 8:12-14

Hebrews 2:14-15

Father obviously did not enjoy the assurance of his salvation that Katy did. Most of mainstream evangelicalism teaches that we can have such assurance. Our Bible Emphasis later in the lesson will discuss this issue as we take an in-depth look at the subject of faith.

4. Suffering, Continued

Katy faces a different season of suffering in this section with her poor health (though her other thorns have not departed!). Review last week's list of Scriptures on suffering (p. 53 of our Bible Study) for applications to Katy's present trials.

5. Comforting Others

Katy writes, "It may be my conceit, but it really does seem as if poor Father was getting a little fond of me. Ever since my own sickness I have felt great sympathy for him, and he feels, no doubt, that I give him something that neither Ernest nor Martha can do, since they were never sick one day in their lives." (p. 155)

Read 2 Corinthians 1:3-7 and apply the passage to Katy's observation.

6. Response to Suffering

A significant conversation about suffering takes place between Katy and Amelia on page 160. Read Hebrews 12:1-15. Note anything you learn about suffering in this passage. Is God's purpose always accomplished in the suffering He allows, or does the result sometimes depend upon our response? How is the answer to this question clearly seen in the contrasting responses of Katy and Amelia to their sufferings?

7. Thanksgiving

Katy counts her blessings on New Year's Day 1841. (pp. 161-162)

Read the following verses to see what God says should continually characterize our hearts.

Psalm 100:4

Philippians 4:6

Colossians 3:16

Colossians 4:2

Hebrews 12:28

The Bible Emphasis: Faith

Katy enjoys an assurance of her salvation that eludes Father. In our Bible Emphasis this week, let us consider what might account for the difference in their levels of peace and joy?

Read the following accounts in the Gospels and note what Jesus commended each person for:

Matthew 8:5-10

Matthew 9:1-8

Matthew 9:20-22

Matthew 15:21-28

Luke 7:36-50

"Faith is the attitude whereby a man abandons all reliance in his own efforts to obtain salvation, be they deeds of piety, of ethical goodness or anything else. **It is the attitude of complete trust in Christ, of reliance in him alone for all that salvation means.**" (*New Bible Dictionary* 366)

Faith is not accepting certain things as true, but trusting a Person, that Person being Christ. The picture of being married to Christ is pertinent here. Think of the difference between saying, "I believe that Jack would make a very good husband." (intellectual belief) and saying, "I, Jill, take, thee, Jack, to be my lawful wedded husband." (placing one's faith – trust – very life – in this man's hands.)

If you struggle with whether or not you have truly made this vow to your Savior, placing your trust in Him alone and His finished work on the Cross to save you from your sin, remember Watchman Nee's parable about FACT, FAITH, and EXPERIENCE. Then read the following FACTS to nurture the assurance of your salvation:

1 John 5:11-13

John 5:24

John 10:27-29

Romans 8:38-39

I am convinced that one key to sensing the assurance of our salvation lies in getting our eyes off ourselves and our unworthiness and onto Christ and His worthiness. Read Hebrews 10:19-23. From where does our confidence come to approach a holy God?

(If you do not understand the reference to the veil in Hebrews 10:20, read Exodus 26:31-33, Matthew 27:50-51, and 2 Corinthians 5:21. The design of the Tabernacle provides a beautiful picture of the way of salvation.)

How are we to draw near to God? (Hebrews 10:22)

Warren Wiersbe comments: "The readers of this epistle (Hebrews) were being tempted to forsake their confession of Jesus Christ by going back to the Old Covenant worship. The writer did not exhort them to hold on to their salvation, *because their security was in Christ and not in themselves* (italics added). Rather, he invited them to hold fast 'the profession [confession] of . . . hope.' (Hebrews 7:25)" ("Be" Series)

How might this invitation to hold fast his profession of hope have helped Father in our story with his fears and doubts? Is it possible that his problem was a temptation to fall back into Old Covenant worship, that is, trying to keep the Law in his own strength in order to *assure himself* of his salvation? Katy writes of Father in our reading for next week:

> **For a sufferer he certainly is who sees a great and good and terrible God who cannot look upon iniquity, and does not see His risen Son, who has paid the debt we owe, and lives to intercede for us before the throne of the Father. (p. 167)**

Do you ever find yourself so overcome with your sinfulness and inability to "keep the Law" that you doubt your salvation and live in fear of judgment from a great and good and terrible God instead of living in joy of relationship with the risen Son? How can we apply Hebrews 10:19-23 to our minds and hearts when we are experiencing this kind of defeat?

Once we can fully embrace the truth that we have been saved *by faith* in the One Who is worthy of our worship, we must also learn to live the rest of our lives *by faith* as well. This involves a second key that will nurture the sense of assurance of our salvation as well.

Read all of Hebrews 11, the great chapter of Scripture known as the Hall of Faith. Here we will see that just as Jesus commended believers of His day for their faith, God's Word also commends men and women from Old Testament times for their faith.

1. How is faith described in Hebrews 11:1-3?

2. Hebrews 11:8 tells us that Abraham's faith resulted in a response of _____.

What does obedience have to do with faith?

How do you see obedience related to faith in other lives of people listed in this chapter?

"In each instance, you will find the same elements of faith:
- God spoke to them through His Word;
- their inner selves were stirred in different ways;
- they obeyed God;
- He bore witness about them." (Wiersbe)

What does obedience have to do with the assurance of one's salvation?

3. In summary, at least two keys are important to experiencing the assurance of our salvation:

- keeping our eyes on Christ's worthiness
- being obedient to His Word

Review Hebrews 12:1-3.

How is this passage a good summary of these two keys?

Who are the "so great a cloud of witnesses"?

What are we to do in the light of their faithful lives?

As we practice obedience, why is it important to keep our eyes on Jesus and to think about His sufferings?

4. Now return to Hebrews 11 for a moment. A friend once said to me, "Well, it must not have been the Lord's will for that family to go to the mission field. They must have misunderstood His leading. Otherwise, their son would not have died in that God-forsaken place." Use Hebrews 11:35b-38 to refute this kind of thinking.

5. Select one person mentioned in this Hebrews 11 Hall of Faith about whom you know little and would like to know more. Use a concordance or other study tools to explore what Scripture has to say about that person. Record your notes below:

Personal Applications

(Remember to record your responses to these two questions in your journal.)

1. Select ONE of the "Treasures from the Story." (See pp. 57-59 of the lesson.)

    *   If God's message brought an eye-opening truth that comforted or encouraged you, respond with gratitude. (DOCTRINE)

    *   If His message convicted you of sin, respond with confession and accept His forgiveness. (REPROOF)

    *   If His message instructed you to take some action, respond with obedience. (CORRECTION AND INSTRUCTION IN RIGHTEOUSNESS)

2. Review the two keys to having assurance of our salvation that we studied in "The Bible Emphasis" this week. Which one do you need to practice more regularly to mature in your faith? How will you begin to practice that key?

Katy Deals with Death

(The closing two lines are to be found upon Mrs. Prentiss' tombstone.)
And by and by, we children
Shall grow into perfect men,
And the loving, patient Master
From school will dismiss us then.

No more tedious lessons,
No more sighing and tears,
But a bound into home immortal,
And blessed, blessed years! (Prentiss 51)

65

Katy Deals with Death

O death, where is thy sting? O grave, where is thy victory? 1 Corinthians 15:55

Treasures from the Story

1. Grieving vs. Complaining

Mrs. Campbell says, "It is *complaining* that dishonors God, not grief."(p. 164) The Bible clearly forbids complaining. It never commands us not to grieve, however; it even instructs us how to grieve.

Read Philippians 2:14-16. Why are we not to complain (murmur and dispute)?

Read 1 Thessalonians 4:13-18. How do we grieve (sorrow) differently from the world? Why can we do this?

2. The Sin of Pride

Katy writes, "How thankful I am that I am as unlike them (Charlie and Amelia) as. ." (p. 170) Read Luke 18:9-14. How does Katy come to realize that she has much in common with the Pharisee of this parable? (pp. 170-172)

How does her sin of pride continue to operate even after God has convicted her that her thoughts toward Amelia and Charlie were sinful? (p. 172)

C.S. Lewis devotes an entire chapter in his classic *Mere Christianity* to the subject of pride. He writes:

> **It is a terrible thing that the worst of all the vices can smuggle itself into the very centre of our religious life. (Note the things that our heroine Katy is proud of!) But you can see why. The other, and less bad, vices come from the devil working on us through our animal nature. But this does not come though our animal nature at all. It comes direct from hell. It is purely spiritual: consequently it is far more subtle and deadly. . . . The devil laughs. He is perfectly content to see you becoming chaste and brave and self-controlled provided, all the time, he is setting up in you the Dictatorship of Pride – just as he would be quite content to see your chilblains cured if he was allowed, in return, to give you cancer. For Pride is spiritual cancer: it eats up the very possibility of love, or contentment, or even common sense. (112.)**

Let us look briefly into the scriptural basis for saying that the sin of pride originated directly from the devil.

Read Isaiah 14:12-14.

Although the immediate reference in Isaiah 14:12-14 is probably to the Assyrian King Sennacherib, most Bible students agree that it is also a description of the fall of Satan himself. (See Luke 10:18) Pride was first revealed when Lucifer attempted to set his throne on high in proud independence of God.

How many times does the "morning star, son of the dawn" use the pronoun 'I' in this passage? The word *pride* is not used here, but write a definition of pride based on this passage.

Read Genesis 3:1-5.

How did the fallen devil entice Adam and Eve in such a way as to infect the entire human race with the sin of pride through the Fall?

A marvelous example of God's dealing with a mighty man of pride is found in Daniel 4. Nebuchadnezzar, King of Babylon, tells the story in his own words of calling Daniel, the righteous Jew, to interpret a disturbing dream he has had. In his explanation, Daniel warns this most powerful man on earth that he will be driven into the wilderness to live with and like the wild animals until he will acknowledge *"that the most High ruleth in the kingdom of men, and giveth it to whomsoever he will."* (Daniel 4:25) Daniel then advises the King: *". . . break off thy sins by righteousness, and thine iniquities by shewing mercy to the poor; if it may be a lengthening of thy tranquility."* (Daniel 4:27)

Read the rest of the story: Daniel 4:28-37.

How does God humble this proud man? What lesson does King Nebuchadnezzar learn?

Read Proverbs 3:34, Proverbs 16:18, James 4:6, and 1 Peter 5:5 and explain how the stories of Lucifer and of Nebuchadnezzar exemplify these verses.

Now read Philippians 2:5-11 for the supreme example of pride's opposite: humility. How did Christ's life (and God's dealings with His Son) exemplify perfect humility and its outcome?

3. Motherhood Modeled

Katy models for us much of excellent motherhood. Read the journal entries on the next page in the left column and match each of them with a Scripture in the right column. Select one Scripture that you want to apply to parenting your children (or grandchildren) or to those God gives you to mother. Write it into your journal. If you are not memorizing the selected Scripture for the week, memorize this one.

Quotation from the story	Scriptures
"I feel ready to sink when I think of the great work God has entrusted to me. But my poor child will learn that he is a sinner only too soon, and before that dreadful day arrives I want to fortify his soul with the only antidote against the misery that knowledge will give him. I want him to see his Redeemer in all His love, and all His beauty, and to love Him with all his heart and soul, and mind and strength." (p. 167) Scripture: _____	**Lamentations 2:19** *Arise, cry out in the night: in the beginning of the watches pour out thine heart like water before the face of the Lord: lift up thy hands toward him for the life of thy young children, that faint for hunger in the top of every street.*
"Dear James! it must be Mother's prayers that have done for him this wondrous work that is usually the slow growth of years; and this is the mother who prays for you, Katy! So take courage!" (p. 169) Scripture: _____	**Proverbs 24:3-4** *Through wisdom is an house builded; and by understanding it is established: 4And by knowledge shall the chambers be filled with all precious and pleasant riches.*
"Here is a sweet, fragrant mouth to kiss; here are two more feet to make music with their pattering about my nursery. Here is a soul to train for God; and the body in which it dwells is worthy all it will cost, since it is the abode of a kingly tenant. I may see less of friends, but I have gained one dearer than them all, to whom, while I minister in Christ's name, I make a willing sacrifice of what little leisure for my own recreation my other darlings had left me. Yes, my precious baby, you are welcome to your mother's heart, welcome to her time, her strength, her health, her most tender cares, to her lifelong prayers! Oh, how rich I am, how truly, how wondrously blest!" (p. 178) Scripture: _____	**Psalm 127-128** *A Song of degrees for Solomon.* *Except the Lord build the house, they labour in vain that build it: except the Lord keep the city, the watchman waketh but in vain. 2It is vain for you to rise up early, to sit up late, to eat the bread of sorrows: for so he giveth his beloved sleep. 3Lo, children are an heritage of the Lord: and the fruit of the womb is his reward. 4As arrows are in the hand of a mighty man; so are children of the youth. 5Happy is the man that hath his quiver full of them: they shall not be ashamed, but they shall speak with the enemies in the gate.* *128:1A Song of degrees.* *Blessed is every one that feareth the Lord; that walketh in his ways. 2For thou shalt eat the labour of thine hands: happy shalt thou be, and it shall be well with thee. 3Thy wife shall be as a fruitful vine by the sides of thine house: thy children like olive plants round about thy table. 4Behold, that thus shall the man be blessed that feareth the Lord. 5The Lord shall bless thee out of Zion: and thou shalt see the good of Jerusalem all the days of thy life. 6Yea, thou shalt see thy children's children, and peace upon Israel.*
"I am so selfish, and it is so hard to practice the very law of love I preach to my children! Yet I want this law to rule and reign in my home, that it may be a little heaven below, and I will not, no, I *will* not, cease praying that it may be such, no matter what it costs me. Poor father! poor old man! I will try to make your home so sweet and homelike to you that when you change it for heaven it shall be but a transition from one bliss to a higher!" (p. 179) Scripture: _____	**Ephesians 6:4** *And, ye fathers, provoke not your children to wrath: but bring them up in the nurture and admonition of the Lord.*

4. The Letter vs. the Spirit

After Father returns to live with Katy and Ernest once more, Katy writes, ". . .she (Mother) sits at my right hand at the table, the living personification of the blessed gospel of good tidings, with Father, opposite, the fading image of the law given by Moses." (p. 184)

Read Exodus 34:29-35 and 2 Corinthians 3:7-18, and explain Katy's contrast between Mother and Father.

Katy also remarks that despite Father's ailments and fits of despair, he is "quiet and gentle, and even loving, and as he sits in his corner, his Bible on his knees, I see how much more he reads the New Testament than he used to do, and that the fourteenth chapter of St. John almost opens to him of itself." (p. 184) What is in John 14 that might interest Father?

The Bible Emphasis: Death

The first mention of death in the Bible occurs in Genesis 2:17 where God warns Adam that he must not eat from the tree of the knowledge of good and evil or else he will die. Read Genesis 2:15-17 and all of Genesis 3.

The entrance of death into the human race was a result of what?

From God's curse pronounced on Adam in Genesis 3:19, we can see that the warning God had given to Adam clearly refers at least to physical death. Why does God now say that the man must not be allowed to eat of the tree of life (See Genesis 3:22) even though this tree had NOT been forbidden in God's original plan?

Do you have any thoughts as to why God's banishment of Adam and Eve from the garden might have been an act of mercy? (This answer is not explicitly given in the text. Put on your thinking cap.)

Now read Romans 5:12-21.   On the chart on the next page, note everything you learn about the two men who are contrasted in this passage.

Adam	Jesus Christ
Romans 5:12	
Romans 5:14	
Romans 5:14	
Romans 5:14	
Romans 5: 15	Romans 5:15
Romans 5:17	Romans 5:17
Romans 5:18	Romans 5:18
Romans 5:19	Romans 5:19

On the basis of your observations of this passage, do you think we are still talking about physical death only?

How do the following verses suggest that death goes far beyond the mere physical decay of our bodies?

Romans 8:6

1 John 3:14

Perhaps we should understand that mortality was the result of Adam's sin, and that the penalty includes both physical and spiritual aspects. (We should) understand death as something that involves the whole

man. Man does not die as a body. He dies as a man, in the totality of his being. He dies as a spiritual and physical being. And the Bible does not put a sharp demarcation between the two aspects. Physical death, then is a fit symbol of, and expression of, and unity with, the deeper death that sin inevitably brings. (*New Bible Dictionary* 273)

Isn't this why Jesus had to come? Read 1 Corinthians 15:12-26. Why is Christ's resurrection absolutely crucial to our faith?

The New Testament relentlessly defines human life, death, and resurrection in light of Jesus' life, death, and resurrection. Thus death is removed from its normal context at the end of life and placed in the very middle of life; in Christ we die and are raised as we commit our lives to Him. (Holman)

As death comes into our own life experience, as it did so often into Katy's, we must line up our thinking and response – even through all the pain – with the clear teachings of Scripture:

1. Physical death is not pretty; it is ugly; we may call it 'natural' but it is not good; it is the enemy; it is the result of sin. (1 Corinthians 15:26; Romans 6:23))

2. The ugliness, the associated suffering, the smells, and all of the horrors that accompany physical death should remind us that this is a mere picture of a deeper reality: spiritual death. (Matthew 23:27; Ephesians 2:1)

3. Jesus Christ has overcome death, both physical and spiritual. Through our relationship with Him, we pass from spiritual death to spiritual life, AND we can, therefore, face our own physical death without fear. (John 5:24; 1 Corinthians 15:35-58)

4. In addition, when our loved ones physically die, if they are in Christ, we can – even in our grief – rejoice, knowing that they are still spiritually alive and eternally safe with the Savior. (1 Thessalonians 4:13-18)

5. The reality of physical and spiritual death should give us a fresh burden for the lost among us, who are dead spiritually and who do not have the hope that we do. (1 Corinthians 9:19-23)

Read John 11.

What is Jesus' stated reason (John 11:15) for raising Lazarus from the dead?

For what other reason might Jesus have performed this miracle, even though Lazarus would eventually die again?

Personal Applications

(Remember to record your responses to these two questions in your journal.)

1. Select ONE of the "Treasures from the Story." (See pp. 67-71 of the lesson.)

    *   If God's message brought an eye-opening truth that comforted or encouraged you, respond with gratitude. (DOCTRINE)

    *   If His message convicted you of sin, respond with confession and accept His forgiveness. (REPROOF)

    *   If His message instructed you to take some action, respond with obedience. (CORRECTION AND INSTRUCTION IN RIGHTEOUSNESS)

2. Re-read the discussion between Katy and Ernest about Amelia's death. (p. 177) Consider these statements made by Ernest:

    "Of course there is but one real preparation for Christian dying, and that is Christian living."

    "I do not recall a single instance where a worldly Christian died a happy, joyful death, in all my practice."

    ". . . we must not forget that God is honored or dishonored by the way a Christian dies, as well as by the way in which he lives."

    "And it gives me positive personal pain to see heirs of the eternal kingdom, made such by the ignominious death of their Lord, go shrinking and weeping to the full possession of their inheritance."

    React to any of these statements by sharing your own experiences, hopes, or fears. If any of your thinking does not line up with the Bible's teaching on death, ask God to help you think biblically about this difficult subject.

Lesson Eight
(Chapters 20-22: pp. 194-220)

Katy Discovers True Peace

"He who knows the secret of endurance will enjoy the greatest peace. Such a one
is conquerer of self, master of the world, a friend of Christ, and an heir of Heaven."
(Thomas a Kempis 71)

Katy Discovers True Peace

Peace I leave with you, my peace I give unto you: not as the world giveth, give I unto you.
Let not your heart be troubled, neither let it be afraid.
John 14:27

Treasures from the Story

1. The Word of God, Reviewed

As Katy grows in Christ, we see the Word of God becoming a primary tool in the shaping of her character. Notice the ways that God's Word impacts her life daily in this week's reading:

A. Doctrine that brings Comfort:

On June 10, 1842, Katy had written, "Yes, we will *give* our children to Him if He asks for them. He shall never have to *snatch* them from us by force." (p. 166) Two summers later she faces a severe testing of that declaration. The Psalms particularly minister to her during this time, bringing her comfort in the midst of her suffering. (pp. 199-200) What teachings about God's character – that is, doctrinal truths - are in the Psalms that can comfort and encourage us when we remind ourselves of those FACTS?

B. Reproof:

After Father's death and Katy's discovery that his habit on holidays had been to fast and pray for them, she again upbraids herself for misinterpreting people's motives. (p. 194) What words from 1 Corinthians 13:5-7 convict her of her sin against this precious man.

C. Correction and Instruction in Righteousness:

Katy writes of her children, "I talk to her of Christ, . . . If I required a little self-denial, I said, cheerfully, 'This is hard, but doing it for our best Friend sweetens it, . . .'" (p. 198) How do we see here and in other places that Katy is obeying the instruction in Ephesians 6:4 and modeling out Proverbs 31:26?

2. True Happiness

Read Proverbs 15:17 and apply to Katy's observation about happiness on p. 202.

3. Growing Up

Read Katy's reflection on page 203, where she confides to her journal that she does not get as much from Dr. Cabot's instruction as she once did. Has Dr. Cabot lost his ability to teach? Or is Katy simply growing up? Read the following Scriptures and apply them to what Katy is learning.

1 Corinthians 11:1

Ephesians 4:11-16

Hebrews 5:11-14 (The writer has just been talking about Melchizedek being a picture of Christ. He apparently believes that his readers may not fully understand what he is talking about.)

2 Peter 3:17-18 (What they already know is that there are false teachers afoot who will distort the Scriptures)

4. An Evangelistic Model

Notice how Katy's role begins to shift here to that of a mentor when she meets Miss Clifford. (pp. 204-208) How does Katy's style of evangelism differ from much of our modern "door-to-door, get'em to pray the prayer" style? Find elements of Katy's approach to Miss Clifford in the following passages of Scripture.

Colossians 4:2-6

2 Timothy 4:2-5

1 Corinthians 9:19-23

5. Honoring Our Spouse With Our Words

Though Ernest often fails to affirm Katy with words - ("He listened in his usual silence, and I longed to hear him say whether I had spoken wisely and well." - p. 208) – notice from Miss Clifford's remarks how he honors her publicly:

- "I see you are just what the doctor boasted you were," . . . (p. 205)

- "I told the doctor the other day that life was nothing but a humbug, and he said he would bring me a remedy against that false notion the next time he came, and you, I suppose, are that remedy," (p. 205)

To apply this principle of honor to ourselves as wives, read Proverbs 31:12 and 23. How might this woman's public words about her husband have contributed to the respect he received at the city gate? Have you spoken of your husband to another person in a way that dishonored him since you were asked this question in Lesson Five?

OBSERVATION: Mother's remarks about female appearances, even to the remark about hair, remind us that our culture's obsession with looks is not entirely modern. Read 1 Peter 3:3-4. Hmmm . . .Apparently, women have been susceptible to this trap in their "instinctive desire to please" (p. 209) for more than just the last two centuries!

6. A Plan of Life

Mother speaks to Miss Clifford about having "a plan of life." (p. 210) Read Matthew 7:24-27.

Who is the wise man? What is the result of his choice of "life plan"?

Who is the foolish man? What is the result of his choice of "life plan"?

Read Luke 14:25-33.

What will it cost us to build our lives according to God's plan?

How is Katy learning this hard lesson?

How are you learning it?

The Bible Emphasis: Peace

After Ethel's birth, Katy writes, "If I were called upon to declare what has been the chief element of my happiness, . . . underneath them all, deeper, stronger than all, lies a peace with God that I can compare to no other joy, which I guard as I would guard hidden treasure, and which must abide even if all other things pass away." (p. 215) How far Katy has come in the twelve years since she received Dr. Cabot's letter! (See Lesson Three – p. 31 of our Bible study – Quotation "e")

Read Matthew 13:44-46. How do Jesus' pictures of the Kingdom of heaven remind you of our insights into having "a plan of life"?

Katy names this treasure "peace with God." Let's explore the theme of peace in God's Word for our Bible Emphasis this week.

Read the following verses from Isaiah and list everything you learn about peace. Then put a star by the three that you think may be prophecies of the long-awaited Messiah. (Don't obsess on this question. There could be more than three that refer to Christ. Ultimately every reference to true Peace is a reference to Him!)

Isaiah 26:3

Isaiah 26:12

Isaiah 32:17

Isaiah 48:18

Isaiah 52:7

Isaiah 53:5

Isaiah 57:2

Isaiah 57:18-19

Isaiah 57:21

Isaiah 59:8

Now read Jesus' words and record what you learn from Him about peace.

Luke 19:41-42

John 14:27

John 16:33

Read the following verses and note how the Trinity is involved in administering peace to us.

Romans 5:1

Romans 8:6

Galatians 5:22-23 (James 3:17-18 is a good cross-reference for these verses)

Read Ephesians 2:11-18. Explain from this passage how peace between men is part of the purpose for which Christ died.

Once we have peace WITH God through a relationship with Christ Jesus, He gives us the peace OF God, and He calls us to peace with men. The vertical relationship with God must be right in order for us to have the inner peace we long for and in order for our horizontal relationships with each other to have any hope of being right. Below are several passages of Scripture. They cover a wide variety of topics, but each one gives us specific instruction in promoting peace. The 1 John verse involves maintaining peace with God once He has saved you. The Philippians passage instructs us concerning inner peace. The remaining verses deal with peace between men. Record what you learn.

1 John 1:9

Philippians 4:6-7

Romans 12:14-21

Romans 14:13-21

1 Corinthians 7:12-16

Colossians 3:12-17

2 Timothy 2:22-26

Hebrews 12:7-13

Personal Applications

(Remember to record your responses to these two questions in your journal.)

1. Select ONE of the "Treasures from the Story." (See pp. 77-79 of the lesson.)

    - If God's message brought an eye-opening truth that comforted or encouraged you, respond with gratitude. (DOCTRINE)

    - If His message convicted you of sin, respond with confession and accept His forgiveness. (REPROOF)

    - If His message instructed you to take some action, respond with obedience. (CORRECTION AND INSTRUCTION IN RIGHTEOUSNESS)

2. a. What aspect of your life most often robs you of inner peace or of peace with others?

    b. What have you learned in your study on peace this week that could increase your "peace quotient"?

Lesson Nine
(Chapters 23-25: pp. 221-249)

Katy Learns Christ: Worship

"*You arouse him (man) to take joy in praising you, for you have made us for yourself, and our heart is restless until it rests in you.*" (*Augustine 45*)

Katy Learns Christ: Worship

Behold, to obey is better than sacrifice, and to hearken than the fat of rams. 1 Samuel 15:22b

Treasures from the Story

1. The Godly Older Woman

After James's death, Katy writes, "I do not know what to say of Mother but that she behaved and quieted herself like a weaned child." (p. 221)

Read Psalm 131 from which Katy's reference comes.

What does being proud or haughty have to do with quieting ourselves before the Lord?

What picture do you have of Mother from reading this Psalm and reflecting on the comparison to a weaned child?

I have found the portraits of godly older women in this story instructive and encouraging as I think about what I want to be like in my latter years. We need to remind ourselves of what the Bible says about age, *not* what the world says. Read the following verses and note the discrepancy between God's view and the world's view of age.

Psalm 92:12-15

Proverbs 16:31

Growing old does not guarantee godly character, but this day, this week, this year, those of you still in your youth are making choices that will determine whether you become a Mrs. Campbell /Mother or whether you become a Mrs. Green.

Katy says that, "My steadfast aim now is to follow in my mother's footsteps; to imitate her cheerfulness, her benevolence, her bright, inspiring ways, and never to rest till in place of my selfish nature I become as full of Christ's love as she became." (p. 224) Would it not be a supreme joy to find this statement in the journal of your grown daughter someday?

Review 1 Corinthians 11:1 and apply to Katy's aim.

2. Two Types of Complaints

Daniel Wilson was an Anglican Bishop in India in the first half of the nineteenth century, according to a footnote (p. 225) in our book. Katy is convicted by his charge "to bear all these things 'as unto God' and 'with the greatest privacy.'" She goes on to lament, ". . .how I have tormented my friends by tedious complaints about (the daily trials of life)!" (p. 225)

Ah, dear sisters, can you relate to Katy's frustration over her slowness in learning to control her tongue, particularly in the complaining area? I certainly can!

Read Numbers 11:1-3. What did God think about the complaints of the Israelites?

Now read the complaints of David (Psalm 142) and of Jeremiah (Lamentations 3:1-26). (We read this passage in Lesson Four when we were studying how to deal with disappointment.) How do the complaints of these men differ from those of the Israelite community in Numbers?

How does Jeremiah's observation in Lamentations 3:25-26 confirm Katy's conviction about her tongue?

According to Paul in Philippians 2:14-16, how might the complaining tongue of a Christian impede her witness?

3. Joy

As I read the discussion between Katy and Helen on pages 226-231, I wanted to haul out the entire book of Philippians to study with you! But later in the lesson, I found another topic that was begging to be the Bible Emphasis for the week.

So . . . just a brief comment on Philippians' theme of joy. Helen's problem is the same as mine: the misbelief that our highest joy comes from our circumstances and from our human relationships rather than from the forgiveness we have in Christ and from a growing, intimate relationship with Him.

Read Philippians 3:7-11. What is Paul's passion?

Read Philippians 4:10-13. How do you think that Paul's passion, stated above, might have taught him the lesson he describes in these verses?

How is Katy closer to imitating Paul's outlook than Helen is? How close are you? (Remember, Paul writes: "Follow my example, as I follow the example of Christ." 1 Corinthians 11:1)

4. Wisdom in Speech

In the midst of this conversation with Helen, Katy displays much wisdom and maturity in the Lord. Read the following verses and explain how Katy models each command as she talks with Helen.

Hebrews 10:24

James 5:16

Colossians 3:12

5. Wisdom in Actions

Helen marvels at Katy's ability to frolic with her children when they come in from school even though she has just been having a most somber conversation. Katy replies, "I think a mother, especially, must *learn* (italics added) to enter into the happy moods of her children at the very moment when her own heart is sad. And it may be as religious an act for her to romp with them at that time as to pray with them at others." (p. 232)

Notice Katy's use of the word *learn*. Earlier she remarks that she has "formed the habit of" (p. 231) giving herself entirely to the children at such moments. Obviously, the ability to rejoice with those who are rejoicing and to mourn with those who are mourning (Romans 12:15) has not come naturally to Katy. Why not? What has to be happening in our hearts in order to have this flexibility? (See Philippians 2:1-7)

Go back to the top of page 12 in Lesson One in our Bible Study. How is Katy carrying out the commands Paul gives in Romans 6 (and also in Romans 8:13)? Whatever does mortifying the deeds of the body have to do with playing with one's children? What does Katy mean by calling the romp a religious act?

6. Hospitality

Katy writes a humorous description of her day on pages 233-236. She exclaims in dismay, "It is nearly five o'clock, and this whole day has been frittered away in the insignificant trifles. It isn't living to live so. Who is the better for my being in the world since six o'clock this morning?" (p. 236) Helen responds with sweet words about the gracefulness of Katy's and Ernest's hospitality.

Read the following verses, noting anything you learn about hospitality.

Romans 12:13-14

Romans 16:23a

1 Timothy 3:2

1 Timothy 5:9-10

Titus 1:6-9

1 Peter 4:7-10

3 John 5-8

If you have acquired tools, do a simple word study on *hospitality* for a surprising insight.

7. The Mind Battle, Still Continued

When Ernest peeks into the room where Katy sits with the children gathered around her, she frets that perhaps he is thinking that she indulges them too much. He replies, "My precious wife, why will you torment yourself with such fancies? (p. 237)

What Scripture verse does Ernest's rebuke call to mind? (Hint: We have looked at this theme several times in our earlier lessons since it applies to a besetting sin of Katy's.)

8. The Wisdom of Fenelon

When Miss Clifford comes to lunch, she brings a book to read aloud to Katy and Helen. The author, Francois Fenelon, was a French mystic and a Christian Ann Landers of sorts. (See editor's footnote on page 233.)

Each woman was struck by a different bit of wisdom in the book. (pp. 240-243) Select a point that particularly spoke to you and explain below. Try to use Scripture in your explanation.

9. Body Life

Katy, Helen, and Miss Clifford have modeled for us in this discussion a beautiful example of true Christian fellowship. Find out the meaning of the word *fellowship* as used in the New Testament by reading the following "one another" commands. (Fellowship is NOT just having lunch together at a restaurant with another Christian although eating together certainly establishes an atmosphere in which it can take place.)

John 13:34

Romans 15:7

Romans 15:14

1 Corinthians 1:10

Galatians 5:13

Ephesians 4:32

Colossians 3:16

1 Thessalonians 5:11

Hebrews 10:24-25

1 Peter 4:9

What elements of fellowship do you see these women exemplifying on pp. 240-245?

Do you have this kind of fellowship with anyone?

10.   Accountability for Our Light

"Why do we waste our lives before we learn how to live?" (p. 246) Katy laments to Ernest. Read his profound response on page 246. Katy later asks herself, "Is there not in my heart some secret reluctance to know the truth, lest that knowledge should call to a higher and a holier life than I have yet lived?" (pp. 246-247) Read Luke 12:47-48 and apply here.

The Bible Emphasis: Worship

The wide variety of lessons that have abounded throughout this precious story are all gradually coming into focus on this one thought: "To learn Christ, this is life!" (Mrs. Campbell – p. 248)

In learning Christ, we learn to become aware of His presence in us and with us continually. Responding to the awareness of the presence of a holy God is what we call worship. Worship, that is, the direct acknowledgment of God, of His nature, attributes, ways and claims, can take the form of an outgoing of the heart in praise and thanksgiving or it can take the form of deeds done in such acknowledgement.

Read the following stories and note how each character responds in worship when he perceives the presence of God. The word *worship* is used only once, but consider any response the person makes as a result of recognizing the presence of God to be worship.

Genesis 28:10-22

Judges 7:7-15

Luke 1:26-55

Each of the three examples we have looked at above involves a personal experience between the individual and God. Worship in the Bible, however, is portrayed not only as a personal experience, but as a corporate experience as well. Corporate worship for the Jews centered around their sacrificial system in the tabernacle and later in the temple. God's people went to the place where God dwelt and there as a community acknowledged His presence with regular blood sacrifices and with the celebration of special holidays such as Passover.

Unfortunately, because of the ritualistic nature of the system, the ceremonies often became empty and meaningless and did not lead to holy living. The prophet Samuel confronted King Saul over his disobedience when God ordered the Israelites to destroy everything in their battle with the Amalekites. Saul offered the excuse that he had saved some of the animals to sacrifice to God. Read Samuel's reply in I Samuel 15:22. What was his point?

After King David committed adultery with Bathsheba and was confronted by the prophet Nathan, he penned his well-known Psalm of confession. Read Psalm 51:16-17. How did David recognize that animal sacrifices do not constitute true worship unless they are offered with a pure heart?

Hypocrisy grew in the sacrificial system as Israel strayed far from the Lord over and over again but continued to practice their outward show of worship century after century. Isaiah addressed this hypocrisy in Isaiah 1:10-17. (This passage is representative of the sentiment expressed by many of the prophets.) What does God say about His people's worship of Him?

Israel ended up being exiled from the Promised Land for their disobedience, though a remnant eventually returned to inhabit it once more. By Jesus' day, the Jews were under Roman rule, but they were still allowed to practice the rituals of their faith and to keep their laws. Unhappily, emptiness and hypocrisy still abounded in the system as we see in several teachings of Jesus. Read the following passages and note what problem of their worship He addresses in each.

Matthew 15:1-9 (See Isaiah 29:13)

Mark 12:28-34

John 4:19-24

Paul echoes the theme of sacrifice in his explanation of the Gospel when he urges the Romans to offer their bodies as living sacrifices BECAUSE of God's mercy to them. Read Romans 12:1-2 and explain what a "reasonable service" is. (Or "spiritual act of worship" or "spiritual service of worship.")

In the light of all this Truth, I want you now to go back and re-read pp. 245b-249t of our story.

When Una lingers near death after a head injury, Katy wrestles with God and then surrenders her "ewe lamb" to Him. At that moment God "who had only lifted the rod to test my faith laid it down." (p. 248) This can only be an allusion to the story of Abraham's sacrifice of his son Isaac. Before we close, we must look at this incredible passage.

Read Genesis 22:1-19.

What does Abraham say he is going to do on the mountain? (Genesis 22:5) This is the very first use of the word *worship* in the Bible!

What does worship have to do with giving your son as a burnt offering?!

May we not only offer lips that praise Him but may we truly put into practice Ernest's words: "Yes, every act of obedience is an act of worship," (p. 246) as we respond to the presence of a holy God in our lives.

Personal Applications

(Remember to record your responses to these two questions in your journal.)

1. Select ONE of the "Treasures from the Story." (See pp. 87-92 of the lesson.)

   - If God's message brought an eye-opening truth that comforted or encouraged you, respond with gratitude. (DOCTRINE)

   - If His message convicted you of sin, respond with confession and accept His forgiveness. (REPROOF)

   - If His message instructed you to take some action, respond with obedience. (CORRECTION AND INSTRUCTION IN RIGHTEOUSNESS)

2. How are you doing in responding to the presence of a holy God in your life, either with a heart of praise and thanksgiving or with deeds?

Lesson Ten
(Chapters 26-27: pp. 250-272)

Katy's Final Lessons to Us

"*As the eye which has gazed at the sun, cannot immediately discern any other object; as the man who has been accustomed to behold the ocean, turns with contempt from a stagnant pool, so the mind which has contemplated eternity, overlooks and despises the things of time.*" (Payson 99)

Katy's Final Lessons to Us

Teach me, O Lord, the way of thy statutes; and I shall keep it unto the end. Give me understanding, and I shall keep thy law; yea, I shall observe it with my whole heart. Make me to go in the path of thy commandments; for therein do I delight. Incline my heart unto thy testimonies, and not to covetousness. Turn away mine eyes from beholding vanity; and quicken thou me in thy way. Psalm 119:33-37

We have reached the last lesson of our journey together as we have sought to "step heavenward" in our walk with Christ. This week's lesson takes on a different design from the previous lessons. Five topics are presented for prayer and meditation, one for each day of study. References to the end of our story are accompanied by pertinent Scriptures. Read a section each day and meditate prayerfully on the Scriptures. Then respond in your journal with gratitude, confession, a commitment to obedience, or a cry for help to the Lord as He deals with your heart.

Day One

Prayer – Part 1

 As Katy grieves over the loss of her friend, Mrs. Campbell, she writes, ".. she has entered as an inspiration into my life, and through all eternity I shall bless God that he gave me that faithful, praying friend. How little they know who languish in what seem useless sickrooms, or amid the restrictions of frail health, what work they do for Christ by the power of saintly living, and by even fragmentary prayers." (p. 250)

Katy also records Mrs. Campbell's description of a mature Christian on pages 250-251. Re-read that description, noting Katy's plea to her: "Dear Mrs. Campbell, pray for me that I may yet wear her mantle!" (She is referring to her mother who fits Mrs. Campbell's description. If you do not understand the allusion to wearing a mantle, read 1 Kings 19:14-21 and 2 Kings 2:1-15.)

Paul writes to the church at Colossus:

Colossians 1:9-14
For this cause we also, since the day we heard it, do not cease to pray for you, and to desire that ye might be filled with the knowledge of his will in all wisdom and spiritual understanding; That ye might walk worthy of the Lord unto all pleasing, being fruitful in every good work, and increasing in the knowledge of God; Strengthened with all might, according to his glorious power, unto all patience and longsuffering with joyfulness; 2Giving thanks unto the Father, which hath made us meet to be partakers of the inheritance of the saints in light: Who hath delivered us from the power of darkness, and hath translated us into the kingdom of his dear Son: In whom we have redemption through his blood, even the forgiveness of sins:

- Do you have a faithful praying friend? If not, ask God to give you one.

- Are you a faithful praying friend to another? If not, ask God to make you one.

- Ask God's forgiveness for faithlessness in prayer for your friends.

- Is Paul's prayer for the Colossians the kind of prayer that you pray for your friends or the kind of prayer request you give to those who pray for you? As I look over my own prayer requests, I find too much longing to have my perceived needs met and too little longing to become like my Master. May we pray for each other like Paul prayed for the Colossians and may we desire this kind of prayer for ourselves.

Prayer – Part 2

Back in Chapter 22, Katy wrote: "I was struck with Ernest's asking in the very first prayer he offered in my presence, after our marriage, that God would help us love each other; I felt that love was the very foundation on which I was built, and that there was no danger that I would ever fall short in giving to my husband all he wanted, in full measure. But as he went on day after day repeating this prayer, and I naturally made it with him, I came to see that this most precious of earthly blessings had been and must be God's gift, and that while we both looked at it in that light, and felt our dependence on Him for it, we might safely encounter together all the assaults made upon us by the world, the flesh and the devil. I believe we owe it to this constant prayer that we have loved each other so uniformly and with such growing comfort in each other; so that our little discords always have ended in fresh accord, and our love has felt conscious of resting on a rock – and that rock was the will of God." (p. 218)

In the last few pages of the book, she writes, "My married life has been a beautiful one. It is true that sin and folly, and sickness and sorrow, have marred its perfection, but it has been adorned by a love which has never faltered. My faults have never alienated Ernest; his faults, for like other human beings he has them, have never overcome my love to him. This has been the gift of God in answer to our constant prayer, that whatever other bereavement we might have to suffer, we might never be deprived of this benediction. It has been the glad secret of a happy marriage, and I wish I could teach it to every human being who enters upon this state that must bring with it the depth of misery, or life's most sacred and mysterious joy." (p. 265)

Perhaps as Ernest and Katy prayed together, Paul's prayer for the Philippians came to mind:

Philippians 1:9-11
And this I (we) *pray, that your* (our) *love may abound yet more and more in knowledge and in all judgment; That ye* (we) *may approve things that are excellent; that* (we) *ye may be sincere and without offence till the day of Christ; Being filled with the fruits of righteousness, which are by Jesus Christ, unto the glory and praise of God.*

- If you are married, have you ever prayed such a prayer for your marriage – "Lord, help us to love each other."?

- It is not too late to begin to pray this prayer today. Philippians 1:9-11 is an excellent model to use. If your husband is open to praying with you, why not share this part of Katy's story with him and ask him to pray with you, regularly.

Day Two

Thought Life

As Katy reflects on her married life during a season of relative ease, she remarks, "How often I have mistaken his (Ernest's) preoccupied demeanor for indifference; how many times I have inwardly accused him of coldness when his whole heart and soul were filled with the solemn problems of life, aye, and of death likewise." (p. 255)

For one last time, Katy addresses her sin of allowing her mind to draw wrong conclusions about another's heart and motives.

Hopefully, some of you have memorized the following verses by now. If not, begin to work on them.

2 Corinthians 10:3-5

For though we walk in the flesh, we do not war after the flesh: (For the weapons of our warfare are not carnal, but mighty through God to the pulling down of strong holds;) Casting down imaginations, and every high thing that exalteth itself against the knowledge of God, and bringing into captivity every thought to the obedience of Christ;

We need to continually evaluate our thought life in the light of God's truth and ask ourselves whether we do not often fall into the same sin that Katy did.

- Consider carefully when you have been guilty in this area.

- Confess the specific instance and accept God's forgiveness.

- Determine that by the power of His Holy Spirit, you will turn away from this kind of thinking.

- Ask Him to help you to think rightly.

Day Three

Children – Part 1

Katy exclaims to Mrs. Brown, "I want to see little children adorning every home, as flowers adorn every meadow and every wayside. I want to see them welcomed to the homes they enter, to see their parents grow less and less selfish, and more and more loving, because they have come. I want to see God's precious gifts accepted, not frowned upon and refused." (p. 256)

Later, after she has been ill for years, she observes about her own children: "I know the state of each soul as far as it can be known, and have every reason to believe that my children all love my Savior and are trying to live for Him. I have learned, at last, not to despise the day of small things (See Zechariah 4:10), to cherish the most tender blossom, and to expect my dear ones to be imperfect before they become perfect Christians. (p. 269)

King Solomon wrote the following songs about home and children:

Psalm 127 and 128
A Song of degrees for Solomon.

Except the Lord build the house, they labour in vain that build it: except the Lord keep the city, the watchman waketh but in vain. It is vain for you to rise up early, to sit up late, to eat the bread of sorrows: for so he giveth his beloved sleep. Lo, children are an heritage of the Lord: and the fruit of the womb is his reward. As arrows are in the hand of a mighty man; so are children of the youth. Happy is the man that hath his quiver full of them: they shall not be ashamed, but they shall speak with the enemies in the gate.

Blessed is every one that feareth the Lord; that walketh in his ways. For thou shalt eat the labour of thine hands: happy shalt thou be, and it shall be well with thee. Thy wife shall be as a fruitful vine by the sides of thine house: thy children like olive plants round about thy table. Behold, that thus shall the man be blessed that feareth the Lord. The Lord shall bless thee out of Zion: and thou shalt see the good of Jerusalem all the days of thy life. Yea, thou shalt see thy children's children, and peace upon Israel.

- Do you think of your children as flowers adorning your home?

- Are you thankful for them?

- Are they making you less selfish (or highlighting your selfishness?)

- Do they know they are accepted by you? By God?

- Do you expect perfection from them, or are you patient and kind, rejoicing in the small glimpses of progress you see in their characters?

Children – Part 2

Katy writes (with some healthy pride, I think): "People ask me how it happens that my children are all so promptly obedient and so happy. As if it were by *chance* that some parents have such children, or *chance* that some have not! I am afraid it is only too true, as some one has remarked, that 'this is the age of obedient parents!' What then will be the future of their children? How can they yield to God who have never been taught to yield to human authority? And how well fitted will they be to rule their own households who have never learned to rule themselves?" (p. 263)

God makes it clear in His Word from the very first page of Genesis that HE is the ultimate authority. Several verses of Scripture below deal with authority lines in a variety of relationships. Note each:

Romans 13:1-2
Let every soul be subject unto the higher powers. For there is no power but of God: the powers that be are ordained of God. Whosoever therefore resisteth the power, resisteth the ordinance of God: and they that resist shall receive to themselves damnation.

1 Timothy 6:1-2
Let as many servants as are under the yoke count their own masters worthy of all honour, that the name of God and his doctrine be not blasphemed. And they that have believing masters, let them not despise them, because they are brethren; but rather do them service, because they are faithful and beloved, partakers of the benefit. These things teach and exhort.

Ephesians 5:24
Therefore as the church is subject unto Christ, so let the wives be to their own husbands in every thing.

Ephesians 6:1
Children, obey your parents in the Lord, for this is right.

God establishes lines of authority for our protection. Society must have structure to exist. If we fail to set reasonable limits for our children, we train them for irresponsible conduct, lawless lives, and even death (See the Proverbs). The child who learns to respect his parents' authority will find it much easier to submit to other earthly authorities and to God's authority as well. Of course, we must always remember that Godlike authority is characterized by a servant's heart.

As He disciplined His disciples for arguing over who was the greatest, Jesus said, **"For whether is greater, he that sitteth at meat, or he that serveth? is not he that sitteth at meat? but I am among you as he that serveth. (Luke 22:27)**

- Are the lines of authority clear in your home? In other words, if you are married, is your husband the head of your household? Do your children know that *you* are the parents and *they* are the children?

- Do your children have a healthy respect for you as their parents?

- Do you lead lovingly rather than with an authoritarian attitude?

Day Four
Eternal Perspectives (in the bad times)

After Helen's dramatic experience with God when "light broke in upon (her) soul," (p. 259), she says, "I fell upon my knees and gave myself up to the sense of His sovereignty for the first time in my life. Then, too, I looked at my 'light affliction' and at the 'weight of glory,' (2 Corinthians 4:17) side by side, and thanked Him that through the one He had revealed to me the other." (p. 259)

Helen's allusion is to Paul's words to the Corinthian church:

2 Corinthians 4:16-18
Wherefore I beseech you, be ye followers of me. For this cause have I sent unto you Timotheus, who is my beloved son, and faithful in the Lord, who shall bring you into remembrance of my ways which be in Christ, as I teach every where in every church. Now some are puffed up, as though I would not come to you.

- Can you look at your present troubles as "light and momentary" as you meditate on God's sovereignty? In order to do this, we must develop an eternal perspective about all of life.

- List your troubles on the left side of the chart on the next page. Now, as Helen did, meditate on some FACTS from Ephesians (right side of chart) about the "eternal glory that far outweighs" those troubles.

LIGHT AND MOMENTARY TROUBLES	ETERNAL GLORY
	Ephesians 1:3-14 (The Message) *How blessed is God! And what a blessing he is! He's the Father of our Master, Jesus Christ, and takes us to the high places of blessing in him. Long before he laid down earth's foundations, he had us in mind, had settled on us as the focus of his love, to be made whole and holy by his love. Long, long ago he decided to adopt us into his family through Jesus Christ. (What pleasure he took in planning this!) He wanted us to enter into the celebration of his lavish gift-giving by the hand of his beloved Son.* *Because of the sacrifice of the Messiah, his blood poured out on the altar of the Cross, we're a free people—free of penalties and punishments chalked up by all our misdeeds. And not just barely free, either. Abundantly free! He thought of everything, provided for everything we could possibly need, letting us in on the plans he took such delight in making. He set it all out before us in Christ, a long-range plan in which everything would be brought together and summed up in him, everything in deepest heaven, everything on planet earth.* *It's in Christ that we find out who we are and what we are living for. Long before we first heard of Christ and got our hopes up, he had his eye on us, had designs on us for glorious living, part of the overall purpose he is working out in everything and everyone. It's in Christ that you, once you heard the truth and believed it (this Message of your salvation), found yourselves home free—signed, sealed, and delivered by the Holy Spirit. This signet from God is the first installment on what's coming, a reminder that we'll get everything God has planned for us, a praising and glorious life.*

- As you look at the two lists together, try to see God revealing His glory to you through the troubles. Record your meditation in your journal.

Day Five

Eternal Perspectives (in the good times)

We must have an eternal perspective whether we are in troubled times or joyful times. On September 20, 1853, Katy writes, "The mornings and evenings are very cool now, while in the middle of the day it is quite hot. Ernest comes to see us very often, under the pretense that he can't trust me with so young a baby! He is so tender and thoughtful, and spoils me so, that this world is very bright to me; I am a little suspicious of it; for I don't want to be so happy in Ernest, or in my children, as to forget for one instant that I am but a pilgrim and a stranger on earth." (p. 264)

Katy's reference to being a pilgrim and stranger comes from the following verses that we studied in Lesson Six.

Hebrews 11:13-16

These (men and women commended for their faith) *all died in faith, not having received the promises, but having seen them afar off, and were persuaded of them, and embraced them, and confessed that they were strangers and pilgrims on the earth. For they that say such things declare plainly that they seek a country. And truly, if they had been mindful of that country from whence they came out, they might have had opportunity to have returned. But now they desire a better country, that is, an heavenly: wherefore God is not ashamed to be called their God: for he hath prepared for them a city.*

Paul also refers to our true home in his letter to the Philippians:

Philippians 3:17-21

Brethren, be followers together of me, and mark them which walk so as ye have us for an ensample. (For many walk, of whom I have told you often, and now tell you even weeping, that they are the enemies of the cross of Christ: Whose end is destruction, whose God is their belly, and whose glory is in their shame, who mind earthly things.) <u>*For our conversation*</u> (citizenship) *is in heaven; from whence also we look for the Saviour, the Lord Jesus Christ: Who shall change our vile body, that it may be fashioned like unto his glorious body, according to the working whereby he is able even to subdue all things unto himself.*

- Why is it easier to forget – or ignore - the FACT of our citizenship when our lives are overflowing with delightful temporal blessings (which, we must remember, are also gifts from God)?

- One way that we can guard our eternal perspective during the "good times" is to cultivate thankful hearts. Ask God to give you a heart that overflows with gratitude for the temporal blessings of the day. (A temporal blessing is anything that could be taken away from you.)

- Ask God to help you to keep a vision of His glory before you always so that your longing for heaven will not be overshadowed by the good gifts He gives you from above to enjoy along the journey.

Precious sisters in Christ, our journey together has come to an end. What a joy it has been to travel with you and Katy through these last ten weeks together! My prayer for you continues to be the same prayer that I began praying for you the first week of our study: *"That the God of our Lord Jesus Christ, the Father of glory, may give unto you the spirit of wisdom and revelation in the knowledge of him: The eyes of your understanding being enlightened; that ye may know what is the hope of his calling, and what the riches of the glory of his inheritance in the saints, And what is the exceeding greatness of his power to us-ward who believe."* (Ephesians 1:17-19)

May God richly bless you as you continue to step heavenward.

A Timeline of Katy's Life

January 15, 1815 – Katherine Mortimer born

October 24, 1831 – Katy's father dies

January 16, 1837 – Katy marries Ernest Elliott

February 25, 1837 – Ernest's mother dies (Ernest's father and sister move in soon after)

October 4, 1838 – Son Ernest, Jr. born

May 1, 1840 – Daughter Una born

February 1843 – Friend Amelia dies

May 1, 1843 – Son Raymond born

July 1, 1843 – Martha, Ernest's sister, marries Mr. Underhill

Fall, 1843 – Katy's mother moves in

Early March 1844 – Ernest's father dies

July 12, 1844 – Ernest, Jr. dies

November 1846 – Daughter Ethel born (She is never mentioned again.)

March 5, 1847 – James, Katy's brother, dies

Late 1847 – Katy's mother dies

Early 1849 – Daughter Daisy born

April 1, 1852 – Dr. Cabot dies

April 16, 1852 – Mrs. Cabot dies

May 13, 1852 – Mrs. Campbell dies

Summer 1853 – Last son born

January 30, 1860 – Last journal entry

Note: Reference made to another son named Walter. I cannot find a record of his birth.